PURPLE Sage
AND OTHER PLEASURES

A SAVORY COLLECTION
BY THE JUNIOR LEAGUE
OF TUCSON, ARIZONA

For additional copies of PURPLE SAGE
AND OTHER PLEASURES please write:

PURPLE SAGE
The Junior League of Tucson, Inc.
2099 East River Road
Tucson, Arizona 85718

Include your return address with your
check payable to Junior League of Tucson, Inc.
in the amount of $18.95 per volume
plus $2.25 postage and handling,
$4.00 if ordering 2 or more books.

First Edition

First Printing, April, 1986

Printed in the United States of America by

Hart Graphics, Inc., Austin, Texas

©Copyright 1986

The Junior League of Tucson, Inc.

Tucson, Arizona

Library of Congress 86-60336

ISBN 0-9616403-0-8

The Junior League of Tucson, Inc.
reaches out to all young women,
regardless of race, color, religion or
national origin, who demonstrate an
interest in and commitment to
voluntarism.

The purpose of this corporation is
exclusively educational and charitable
and is to promote voluntarism;
to develop the potential of its
members for voluntary participation in
community affairs; and to demonstrate
effectiveness of trained volunteers.

PURPLE SAGE AND OTHER PLEASURES

Chairman	**Cynnie Ochoa**
Secretary	**Debby Rosenberg Kennedy**
Treasurer	**Ellen Hickle**
Editors	**Sandra Rothschild**
	Carol Levine
Recipe Chairman	**Carol Wood Davis**
Testing Coordinators	**Sandra Price Witthoft**
	Paula Mazzocco
Marketing Chairman	**Nancy Miniat**
Computer	**Terri Bower**
Art Chairman	**Debby Rosenberg Kennedy**
Wine Selection	**Jeff Perkins,** *Vintage Selections, Ltd.*
	Charles Rolle
Foreword	**Barbara Kraus**
Contract Liaison	**Barbara Kraus**
Sustaining Advisor	**Ann Hand**

TESTING CHAIRMEN

Hors d'oeuvres	**Felice Jarrold**
Soups	**Debby Johnson**
Salads	**Kim Metz**
Seafood	**Nancy Quebedeaux**
Poultry	**Brenda Wilson**
Meats	**Judy Davidson**
Vegetables	**Kay McLoughlin**
Eggs	**Cynthia Ricker**
Rice & Pasta	**Paula Mazzocco**
Breads	**Debby Johnson**
Sauces	**Bonnie Mehl**
Casseroles	**Nancy Miniat**
Southwestern	**Linda Jackson**
	Bonnie Mehl
Desserts	**Julie Rolle**

ART COMMITTEE

Debby Rosenberg Kennedy

Ellen Hickle

Christy Long

MARKETING COMMITTEE

Nancy Miniat

Susan Flynn

Laury Browning

Cynthia Ricker

Kim Metz

Ellen Hickle

Debby Rosenberg Kennedy

Book Design · Kimura/Bingham Advertising Design   Illustrations · Angela Simon

The West. The Old Pueblo. Mountains.
Desert. Cactus. *Riders of the Purple Sage*. The
brilliant sunset in the desert. The serene twilight
that follows. These images bring forth the
moods, colors, and flavors of Tucson.

As the sun goes down behind the
mountains, the western skies become brilliant
with pastels. The desert flora adopt these hues.
The Tucson twilight reflects the heart and
romance of the West.

Life happens at a different pace here in the
West; the climate is inducive to more time to
enjoy the good things in life . . . including the art
of cooking and enjoying food.

Tucson, this great city, has become a
melting pot of cultures and gastronomic delights.
Splendid European dishes that have found their
way here via immigrants and pioneers have
been added to the wonderful regional foods
from our Mexican and Native American cultures.

These special recipes have been refined and
perfected through the years. In this cookbook,
The Junior League of Tucson endeavors to
capture the essence of desert flavors and savory
delights which abound here. It represents a
growing sophistication which is characteristic of
Tucson while retaining it original heritage and
charm. With *Purple Sage and Other Pleasures*, you
can create the mood and flavor of the Southwest.

TABLE OF CONTENTS

HORS D'OEUVRES

Beginning Pleasures

SAGE PUFFS

PREPARATION TIME: *20 minutes plus sitting time*
YIELD: *6 servings*

1	tablespoon butter
½	cup water
½	cup flour
	Salt and pepper to taste
¼	cup milk
1	egg white
	Oil
3	dozen fresh sage leaves, washed and dried

In small saucepan, combine butter and water. Heat until butter melts. Set aside. Place flour, salt and pepper in a bowl. Whisk in butter-water mixture and milk. Cover and let stand at room temperature for 1 hour. Beat egg white until stiff but not dry. Gently fold into batter. Dip sage leaves in batter, one at a time, and drop into 1 inch of heated oil in large skillet. Do not crowd leaves. Fry until puffs are golden brown, turning once. Drain on paper towel. Keep warm in 300 degree oven until all have been fried.

GARLIC BOWS

PREPARATION TIME: *20 minutes*
YIELD: *40 bows*

1	7.5-ounce can refrigerator buttermilk biscuits
½	cup oil
½	cup grated Parmesan cheese
½	clove garlic, minced
1	tablespoon minced parsley
1	tablespoon oregano
½	teaspoon white pepper

Cut each biscuit into fourths. Roll into thin strips about 3 inches long. Tie each strip into a knot. Bake on an ungreased baking sheet at 475 degrees for 6 minutes. While bows are baking, mix together oil, Parmesan cheese, garlic, parsley, oregano and pepper. As soon as bows are taken from oven, toss them in seasoned oil.

May be frozen. Defrost by baking for 5 minutes at 350 degrees.

ASPARAGUS CANAPÉS

PREPARATION TIME: *20-30 minutes*
YIELD: *10-12 servings*

1 **1-pound loaf white bread, thinly sliced**
4 **ounces Roquefort cheese**
1 **3-ounce package cream cheese, softened**
1 **egg, beaten**
1 **tablespoon mayonnaise**
1 **15-ounce can asparagus**
2 **cups butter, melted**

Cut crusts from bread. Flatten each slice with a rolling pin. Set aside. Mix together cheeses, egg and mayonnaise. Spread mixture on each slice of bread. Top each slice of bread with one asparagus spear. Roll up and cut into three pieces. Brush each piece with melted butter and bake at 350 degrees until lightly browned, about 15 minutes. Serve warm.

May be frozen on a baking sheet and then stored in a covered container. Do not defrost before baking. Brush with melted butter just before baking.
An elegant appetizer when arranged on a gleaming silver tray with a fresh flower garnish.

AVOCADO BOATS

PREPARATION TIME: *5 minutes*
YIELD: *6 servings*

2 **tablespoons ketchup**
2 **tablespoons Worcestershire sauce**
2 **tablespoons lemon juice**
2 **tablespoons butter**
2 **tablespoons sugar**
3 **avocados, halved, peeled and pitted**

Mix ketchup, Worcestershire sauce, lemon juice, butter and sugar together in a saucepan. Heat, but do not boil. Fill avocado wells with sauce and serve on a bed of lettuce.

ORIENTAL STUFFED MUSHROOMS

PREPARATION TIME: *45 minutes*
YIELD: *12 servings*

24 fresh mushrooms (about 1 pound)	Wash mushrooms and pat dry.

STUFFING

½ pound lean ground pork	Remove stems and reserve. Set aside caps. Finely chop stems and combine with pork, water chestnuts, celery, scallions and garlic. Add cornstarch, ginger, sherry, soy sauce and egg white. Mix well. Mound filling into reserved mushroom caps. Set aside and prepare batter.
¼ cup finely chopped water chestnuts	
1 celery stalk, finely chopped	
3 scallions, finely chopped	
1 clove garlic, crushed	
1 teaspoon cornstarch	
1 teaspoon grated fresh ginger	
2 teaspoons dry sherry	
1 teaspoon soy sauce	
1 egg white	

BATTER

½ cup cornstarch	Combine all batter ingredients and mix well.
½ cup flour	
1½ teaspoons baking powder	
½ teaspoon salt	
⅓ cup milk	
⅓ cup water	

½ cup flour	Roll filled mushroom caps in ½ cup flour to coat, then dip caps in prepared batter. In pan or wok, heat oil to 375 degrees. Deep fry 5-6 minutes. Drain on absorbent paper. Serve with Oriental Dipping Sauce.
Oil for frying	
Oriental Dipping Sauce*	

*See recipe for Oriental Dipping Sauce on page 11.

ORIENTAL DIPPING SAUCE

PREPARATION TIME: *30 minutes*
YIELD: *½ cup*

2½ teaspoons cider vinegar

⅓ cup ketchup

1 teaspoon soy sauce

2½ teaspoons sugar

1-2 drops Tabasco sauce

Combine all ingredients in small saucepan. Simmer slowly until thick and dark colored, about 30 minutes.

Perfect with any oriental appetizer, such as Oriental Stuffed Mushrooms or Crab Puffs.

CURRIED OLIVES

PREPARATION TIME: *15-20 minutes plus marinating time*
YIELD: *About 1½ cups*

1 tablespoon minced onion

2 tablespoons lemon juice

1 tablespoon curry powder

½ cup oil

1 16-ounce jar pimento-stuffed green olives

Combine onion and lemon juice and let stand for 5 minutes. Add curry powder and slowly beat in oil. Keeping olives in jar, pour off all liquid. Pour curry mixture over olives, cover jar and shake. Refrigerate olives for at least three days before serving.

Decorative jars of Curried Olives make welcome gifts.

SPINACH ROLL-UPS

PREPARATION TIME: *15 minutes plus rising time*
YIELD: *12 servings*

1 10-ounce package frozen chopped spinach, thawed and squeezed dry

½ cup grated Monterey Jack cheese

1 egg, beaten

2 tablespoons minced onion

1 1-pound loaf frozen bread dough, thawed

3 tablespoons butter, melted

4 tablespoons freshly grated Parmesan cheese

Mix together spinach, Monterey Jack cheese, egg and onion. Set aside. Roll out bread dough to a 16 x 16-inch square. Spread spinach mixture over dough and roll up like a jelly roll. Brush half of melted butter in bottom of a 9 x 13-inch glass pan. Sprinkle with half the Parmesan cheese. Cut the spinach roll in ½-inch slices and place in prepared pan. Brush with remaining butter and sprinkle with remaining Parmesan. Let rise until doubled. Bake at 350 degrees for 20 minutes.

EGGPLANT CAVIAR

PREPARATION TIME: *1 hour, 5 minutes*
YIELD: *2 cups*

1 medium eggplant

2 teaspoons olive oil

1 medium onion, chopped

1 medium green bell pepper, chopped

1 teaspoon white vinegar

1 6-ounce can tomato paste

1 teaspoon powdered sugar

Salt and pepper to taste

Bake eggplant at 350 degrees until soft and shriveled, about 45 minutes. Remove from oven and let cool. Remove skin and chop pulp. In medium skillet, heat oil and sauté onion and green bell pepper until soft. Add eggplant and remaining ingredients. Simmer, uncovered, 20 minutes. Serve hot or cold.

Delicious on small rounds of pumpernickel bread.

BAKED BRIE

PREPARATION TIME: *20 minutes*
YIELD: *20-24 servings*

1 2-pound whole firm wheel of Brie

2 tablespoons butter, melted

1 cup pecan or walnut halves, or whole almonds

1-2 apples, cored and cut into wedges

1-2 pears, cored and cut into wedges

Place cheese in round, shallow oven-proof serving dish. Brush with melted butter. Arrange nuts on top. Bake at 350 degrees until cheese just starts to melt, about 10-12 minutes. Serve in baking dish on a warming tray, with apple and pear wedges as scoops.

CHEESE AND OLIVE TOASTS

PREPARATION TIME: *20 minutes*
YIELD: *8-10 servings*

1 cup grated sharp Cheddar cheese

1 4½-ounce can sliced ripe olives, drained

3 scallions, finely chopped

½ cup mayonnaise

¾ teaspoon curry powder

20-24 ½-inch thick slices long, narrow French bread, lightly toasted on one side

In small bowl, combine cheese, olives and scallions. Set aside. Mix mayonnaise and curry powder together. Fold in cheese mixture. Spread on untoasted sides of French bread slices and broil until bubbly.

Delicious and easy to prepare. Great for unexpected guests.

13

CHEESED BREAD CUBES

PREPARATION TIME: *30 minutes plus chilling time*
YIELD: *10-12 servings*

1	**1-pound loaf day-old white bread, unsliced**
½	**cup butter**
1	**cup grated sharp Cheddar cheese**
1	**3-ounce package cream cheese**
⅛	**teaspoon red pepper (cayenne)**
2	**egg whites**

Remove crusts from bread and discard. Cut bread into 1½-inch cubes. Set aside. Melt butter in heavy-bottomed saucepan. Add cheeses and stir over low heat until mixture is melted and smooth. Stir in red pepper. Beat egg whites until stiff. Fold into the melted cheese mixture. Dip each bread cube into cheese mixture, coating thoroughly. Place on baking sheet and refrigerate overnight, or freeze for future use. Bake at 375 degrees for 10-15 minutes. The cubes will puff. Serve hot.

SESAME CHEESE STICKS

PREPARATION TIME: *20 minutes*
YIELD: *50 servings*

1	**cup flour**
½	**teaspoon salt**
⅛	**teaspoon red pepper (cayenne)**
¼	**pound butter, softened**
½	**cup grated sharp Cheddar cheese**
1-2	**tablespoons milk**
¼	**cup sesame seeds**

Sift together flour, salt and red pepper. Add butter and blend well. Mix in cheese. Gradually add enough milk to make a cohesive dough. On lightly floured surface, roll out dough to ¾-inch thickness. Sprinkle with sesame seeds and lightly roll them into the dough. Cut dough into strips ½-inch wide and 2 inches long. Bake on ungreased baking sheet at 400 degrees until golden brown and crisp, about 8-10 minutes.

A delicious accompaniment for salads or cocktails.

HERB CHEESE SPREAD

PREPARATION TIME: *10 minutes plus chilling time*
YIELD: *10-12 servings*

2 **cloves garlic**	Finely chop garlic in food processor. Add all remaining ingredients and blend until smooth. Place in crock and chill to let flavors blend.
8 **ounces whipped butter, softened**	
2 **8-ounce packages cream cheese, softened**	
1 **teaspoon oregano**	
1 **tablespoon minced parsley**	
¼ **teaspoon thyme**	
¼ **teaspoon dill**	
¼ **teaspoon basil**	
¼ **teaspoon marjoram**	
1 **teaspoon pepper**	

Small crocks of this cheese spread make unique gifts.

SWISS CHEESE DIABLE

PREPARATION TIME: *10 minutes plus chilling time*
YIELD: *8-10 servings*

6 **ounces Swiss cheese, finely grated**	Combine all ingredients and chill for at least two hours. Serve on a bed of lettuce leaves.
4 **hard boiled eggs, finely chopped**	
⅓ **cup sour cream**	
1 **teaspoon dry mustard**	
1 **teaspoon cream-style horseradish**	
½ **teaspoon salt**	
¼ **teaspoon pepper**	
Lettuce leaves	

This tangy cheese spread is delicious on crackers or celery sticks.

CRAB PUFFS

PREPARATION TIME: *30 minutes*
YIELD: *8-10 servings*

½	pound crab meat
1	8-ounce package cream cheese, softened
2	tablespoons dry bread crumbs
2	drops sesame oil
2	scallions, finely chopped
½	clove garlic, crushed
1	1-pound package wonton wrappers
	Peanut oil for frying
	Oriental Dipping Sauce*

Combine crab meat, cream cheese, bread crumbs, sesame oil, scallions and garlic. Mix well. Place 1 teaspoonful of filling in center of each wonton. Fold over one corner to center. Moisten the other corners with water and fold into center, one by one. Press edges to seal. Pour enough peanut oil into a wok or deep fat fryer to float wontons. Heat oil to 375 degrees. Deep fry each puff until golden brown, about 3 minutes. Drain on absorbent paper. Serve with Oriental Dipping Sauce.

See recipe for Oriental Dipping Sauce on page 11.

HOT CLAM DIP

PREPARATION TIME: *3 hours, 20 minutes*
YIELD: *10-12 servings*

2	8-ounce packages cream cheese, softened
1	16-ounce carton sour cream
2	6½-ounce cans minced clams, drained
8	scallions, finely chopped
1	tablespoon Worcestershire sauce
1	clove garlic, minced
2-3	drops Tabasco sauce
	Round loaf unsliced French or sourdough bread
	Armenian cracker bread

Mix together cream cheese, sour cream, clams, scallions, Worcestershire sauce, garlic and Tabasco sauce. Set aside while preparing bread. Cut top off loaf of bread and hollow out, being careful not to puncture crust. Fill bread with clam mixture. Wrap loaf in aluminum foil and bake at 300 degrees for 3 hours. Serve hot with Armenian cracker bread.

Yes, it really does bake for three hours!

PATIO SHRIMP

PREPARATION TIME: *30 minutes*
YIELD: *4-6 servings*

¾	**cup butter**
1	**bay leaf**
¼	**cup lemon juice**
1	**clove garlic, crushed**
1	**teaspoon red pepper (cayenne)**
½	**cup water**
1	**pound medium shrimp in shells (about 26-30 shrimp)**
	Crusty bread

Combine butter, bay leaf, lemon juice, garlic, red pepper and water in saucepan and simmer 10 minutes. Arrange shrimp in a single layer in baking dish and cover with sauce. Bake at 350 degrees until shrimp turn pink and curl, about 20 minutes. Remove bay leaf. Serve hot with crusty bread to soak up juices.

This is a messy but wonderful way to serve shrimp. It is fantastic served on the patio with lots of bread to sop up the juices, big napkins for messy hands from peeling the shrimp and icy white wine to quench the thirst.

SALMON PÂTÉ

PREPARATION TIME: *10 minutes plus chilling time*
YIELD: *6-8 servings*

1	**8-ounce package cream cheese, softened**
1	**tablespoon lemon juice**
2	**teaspoons grated onion**
¼	**teaspoon Liquid Smoke**
1	**teaspoon prepared horseradish**
1	**13-ounce can pink salmon**
½	**cup finely chopped pecans**
3	**tablespoons finely chopped fresh parsley**

Combine cream cheese, lemon juice, onion, liquid smoke and horseradish. Drain and flake salmon and add to mixture. Mix well. Shape into log and roll in pecans and parsley. Chill.

SHRIMP MOUSSE

PREPARATION TIME: *15 minutes plus chilling time*
YIELD: *8-10 servings*

1	**envelope unflavored gelatin**
½	**cup water**
1	**cup Creamed Soup Base***
2	**tablespoons tomato paste**
1	**cup mayonnaise**
1	**8-ounce package cream cheese, softened**
½	**cup green bell pepper, chopped (about ½ pepper)**
1½	**cups chopped celery (about 3 stalks)**
½	**cup chopped onion (about ½ onion)**
½	**pound cooked shrimp, chopped**

Soften gelatin in water. In small saucepan, heat soup base and tomato paste. Stir in gelatin until dissolved. Cool. Cream together mayonnaise and cream cheese and add to saucepan. Stir in vegetables and shrimp. Mix well. Pour into mold and chill.

One 15-ounce can salmon or 12 ounces crab meat can be substituted for shrimp.
To make unmolding easier, "grease" mold with mayonnaise. When ready, invert mold onto serving plate and wrap mold with warm towel for 1 minute. Shake gently. If mousse has been molded into the shape of a fish, garnish with thinly sliced radishes for scales, ripe olive slices for eyes and pimento for mouth.
See recipe for Creamed Soup Base on page 37.

SEVICHE SANTA CRUZ

PREPARATION TIME: *10 minutes plus marinating time*
YIELD: *6-8 servings*

1 **pound red snapper, diced**	Place fish in glass dish with lemon juice. Cover and refrigerate overnight. Turn once or twice. Three to four hours before serving, add scallions, jalapeño, tomatoes, cilantro, olive oil and wine to the marinating fish. Chill well. Just before serving, fold in avocado.
¾ **cup lemon juice**	
3 **scallions, finely diced**	
1 **jalapeño pepper, finely diced**	
2 **tomatoes, peeled and chopped**	
1 **tablespoon minced cilantro**	
4 **tablespoons olive oil**	
2 **tablespoons dry white wine**	
1 **avocado, peeled and chopped**	

The acid in the lemon juice will "cook" the fish. It can be served as a dip with tortilla chips or spooned into sorbet glasses and served as a first course before a formal dinner.

CHICKEN DIJON BITES

PREPARATION TIME: *20 minutes*
YIELD: *12 servings*

2 **whole chicken breasts, skinned and boned**	Cut chicken into 1-inch cubes and sauté in butter until lightly browned, about 10 minutes. Stir in mustard, garlic, parsley and lemon juice. Cook a few minutes longer. Sprinkle with bread crumbs and Parmesan cheese and toss.
4 **tablespoons butter**	
3 **teaspoons Dijon mustard**	
1 **clove garlic, crushed**	
1 **tablespoon minced parsley**	
1 **tablespoon lemon juice**	
¼ **cup dry bread crumbs**	
½ **cup grated Parmesan cheese**	

CHINESE GINGER RIBS

PREPARATION TIME: *1 hour, 30 minutes plus marinating time*
YIELD: *6 servings*

RIBS
6 pounds baby-back pork ribs

1 medium onion, chopped

3 whole cloves

1 bay leaf

1 large celery stalk and top, chopped

1¼ teaspoons thyme

3 drops Tabasco sauce

¼ teaspoon pepper

Place ribs in large pot. Cover with cold water. Bring to a boil and skim as needed. Add onion, cloves, bay leaf, celery, thyme, Tabasco sauce and pepper. Return pot to a boil, reduce heat and simmer, covered, 45 minutes. Drain. While still warm, add ribs to marinade.

MARINADE
1 cup soy sauce

1 cup ketchup

⅔ cup chicken broth

½ cup brown sugar

5 tablespoons grated fresh ginger

3 drops Tabasco sauce

Combine all ingredients for marinade in large, closeable container or heavy plastic bag. Add ribs. Close container and refrigerate overnight.

BARBECUE RUB
4 tablespoons sugar

¾ teaspoon salt

½ teaspoon paprika

½ teaspoon tumeric

½ teaspoon celery seed

¼ teaspoon dry mustard

Combine all ingredients for barbecue rub in small bowl and set aside. Remove ribs from marinade and pat dry. Save remaining marinade. Rub ribs well with barbecue rub. Grill ribs over hot mesquite coals or bake at 350 degrees until ribs are nicely browned, about 45 minutes. Baste frequently with reserved marinade. Cut into serving portions.

Lots of ingredients, but very little effort and a fantastic oriental taste!

FILLED CRESCENTS

PREPARATION TIME: *30-45 minutes*
YIELD: *50 servings*

CRUST
1 **3-ounce package cream cheese, softened**

½ **cup butter, softened**

1-2 **drops Tabasco sauce**

¼ **teaspoon salt**

1 **tablespoon sesame seeds, toasted**

¼ **cup grated Parmesan cheese**

1 **cup flour**

FILLING
1 **cup finely chopped ham, turkey or crab**

⅓ **cup sour cream**

1 **teaspoon Dijon mustard**

Beat together cream cheese, butter, Tabasco sauce, salt and sesame seeds until well blended. Add Parmesan cheese and flour and mix well. Chill dough while preparing filling.
Mix together ham, sour cream and mustard. On floured surface, roll chilled dough very thin and cut into circles about 2½ inches in diameter. Place ½ teaspoon of filling on one side of each circle. Moisten edges and fold over to make half circles. Press edges firmly together and place on a baking sheet. Bake at 450 degrees until lightly browned, about 8-10 minutes. Serve warm.

The dough must be well chilled to roll properly.

ROBUST PÂTÉ

PREPARATION TIME: *20 minutes plus chilling time*
YIELD: *8-10 servings*

1 **pound chicken livers**

3 **scallions, finely chopped**

1 **clove garlic, crushed**

4 **tablespoons butter**

1 **tablespoon cognac**

1 **teaspoon Worcestershire sauce**

2 **drops Tabasco sauce**

Salt to taste

1 **hard boiled egg (optional)**

French bread slices

Simmer chicken livers in water 12-15 minutes. Meanwhile, sauté scallions and garlic in butter until soft. When livers are cooked, drain off water, put livers in blender or food processor and combine with scallions and garlic, cognac, Worcestershire sauce and Tabasco sauce. Blend until smooth. Add salt if needed. Scrape pâté into a bowl or crock and chill several hours to allow flavors to blend and mellow. To serve, garnish with grated hard boiled egg. Serve with French bread slices.

MANDARIN-STYLE POT STICKERS

PREPARATION TIME: *2 hours*
YIELD: *40 servings*

FILLING

2	cups Chinese cabbage, finely chopped
½	pound ground beef or pork
1	4½-ounce can shrimp, drained and chopped
1	4-ounce can chopped mushrooms, drained
2	tablespoons chopped onion
2	tablespoons soy sauce
2	teaspoons sesame oil
1	teaspoon salt
1	teaspoon ginger

DOUGH

3	cups flour
½	teaspoon salt
1	cup boiling water
⅓	cup cold water
¼	cup flour

DIPPING SAUCE

3	tablespoons soy sauce
3	tablespoons white vinegar
	Oil
	Water

Place cabbage in paper towels to remove moisture. Combine cabbage, meat, shrimp, mushrooms, onion, 2 tablespoons soy sauce, sesame oil, 1 teaspoon salt and ginger. Cover and chill thoroughly. To prepare dough, mix together 3 cups flour and ½ teaspoon salt. Slowly add boiling water. Stir well. Add ⅓ cup cold water. Blend well. When dough cools, place on well-floured surface. Knead in remaining ¼ cup flour. Knead entire mixture 8-10 minutes. Place in covered bowl and let rest 15-20 minutes. Combine 3 tablespoons soy sauce and vinegar for dipping sauce. Turn dough out onto floured surface and divide into fourths. Roll each fourth to ⅛-inch thickness. Cut dough into 3-inch rounds. Reroll dough as needed to make at least 40 rounds. Spoon 1 tablespoon filling in center of each round. Fold each in half across filling. Pinch edges to seal. Press gently to slightly flatten bottom. Repeat with each round. Cover all dumplings with dry towel. In large skillet, heat 2 tablespoons oil until very hot. Set about 10 dumplings, pinched edges up, in skillet (dumplings should not touch). Cook 1 minute or until bottoms are lightly browned. Add ⅔ cup water. Cover skillet and cook 10 minutes. Uncover and cook until all water evaporates, 2 to 3 minutes. Add 1 tablespoon oil, coat pan and cook, uncovered, 1 minute more. Remove from pan and keep warm. Repeat process for remaining dumplings.

SPICY CHICKEN STICKS

PREPARATION TIME: *30 minutes plus marinating time*
YIELD: *8-10 servings*

¼ **cup soy sauce**

2 **tablespoons dry white wine**

2 **tablespoons lemon juice**

¼ **teaspoon Tabasco sauce**

3 **scallions, finely chopped**

1 **clove garlic, crushed**

20-24 chicken wing drumettes*

Combine soy sauce, wine, lemon juice, Tabasco sauce, scallions and garlic. Pour over chicken drumettes and marinate overnight in refrigerator. Remove drumettes from marinade. Broil 8-10 inches from heat for 10 minutes. Turn drumettes and broil 10 minutes more.

*A drumette is the largest section of a chicken wing.

CURRY DIP

PREPARATION TIME: *5 minutes plus overnight*
YIELD: *1 cup*

1 **cup mayonnaise**

½ **clove garlic, crushed**

1 **teaspoon curry powder**

1 **teaspoon grated onion**

1 **teaspoon prepared horseradish**

1 **teaspoon tarragon vinegar**

Combine all ingredients and chill overnight.

Arrange crudités in large basket and present dip in a hollowed-out red cabbage.

SOUPS

Pleasures du Jour

CREAM OF BROCCOLI SOUP

PREPARATION TIME: *45 minutes*
YIELD: *6 1-cup servings*

1 large bunch broccoli, cut into small pieces

2 cloves garlic, quartered

2 tablespoons butter

1 tablespoon olive oil

3 cups beef broth

1½ cups light cream

3 egg yolks, slightly beaten

Salt and white pepper to taste

In large skillet or heavy saucepan, sauté broccoli pieces and garlic in butter and olive oil until limp and tender, about 10 minutes. Add broth and cook 20 minutes. Strain and reserve broth. Place garlic and broccoli in blender or food processor. Purée. Stir into reserved broth. In small bowl, whisk cream and egg yolks together. Stir 1 cup hot soup into this mixture. Return entire mixture to remaining soup. Cook and stir over low heat until thick. Season to taste with salt and pepper.

CREAM OF CAULIFLOWER SOUP

PREPARATION TIME: *45 minutes*
YIELD: *4 1-cup servings*

¼ cup chopped onion

½ cup chopped celery stalks and leaves

2 tablespoons butter

1 head cauliflower, washed and cut into pieces

¼ cup butter

½ cup flour

Salt to taste

¼ cup milk or cream

4 egg yolks, beaten (optional)

Parsley, nutmeg, paprika or chopped hard boiled egg for garnish

Sauté onion and celery in butter until translucent. Set aside. Place cauliflower in saucepan with enough water to cover. Simmer until tender. Drain and save cooking water. Set aside a few flowerettes. In blender, combine cauliflower, onions, celery and enough cooking water to blend until smooth. Melt ¼ cup butter in saucepan. Whisk in flour and cook for about 5 minutes. Add 2 cups cooking water. Simmer until thickened, stirring with whisk. Add puréed vegetables. Salt to taste. Just before serving, add milk or cream. Heat to serving temperature, but do not boil. For added richness, stir small amount of soup into egg yolks and add to soup. To serve, place a few flowerettes in each bowl and add soup. Garnish with nutmeg, paprika, parsley or hard boiled egg.

CREAM OF MUSHROOM SOUP

PREPARATION TIME: *1 hour*
YIELD: *6 1-cup servings*

1 pound fresh mushrooms

4 cups chicken broth

2 tablespoons butter

2 tablespoons flour

2 tablespoons sherry

2 cups heavy cream

1½ teaspoons salt

Wipe mushrooms clean (do not wash, as mushrooms retain liquid). Remove mushroom stems. Slice mushroom caps and set aside. Add stems to broth. Simmer for 30 minutes. Strain broth. Discard stems. Make a roux with butter and flour. Bring broth to a boil and whisk in roux. Stir well until slightly thickened. Add sliced caps and simmer 8-10 minutes. Heat cream. Add sherry and heated cream to soup. Heat thoroughly. Add salt.

DOZEN BEAN POT SOUP MIX

PREPARATION TIME: *15 minutes*
YIELD: *15 2-cup packages*

2¼ cups lentils

2¼ cups baby limas

2¼ cups regular limas

2¼ cups black-eyed peas

2¼ cups kidney beans

2¼ cups split peas

2¼ cups great northern beans

2¼ cups pinto beans

2¼ cups red beans

2¼ cups white beans

2¼ cups navy beans

2¼ cups black beans

2¼ cups barley

15 chili pods (1 for each 2-cup package)

Combine all beans in a HUGE bowl or pot. Mix with hands. Fill 2-cup containers with dry bean mixture. Attach Dozen Bean Pot Soup recipe.

Cover jar lids with bright fabrics for a colorful gift.

DOZEN BEAN POT SOUP

PREPARATION TIME: *4 hours, 20 minutes*
YIELD: *8 1-cup servings*

2 cups Dozen Bean Pot Soup Mix
1 quart water
1 ham hock or 2 cups cubed ham
2 cups tomato juice
2 cups chicken broth
1 large onion, chopped
1 clove garlic, minced
3 tablespoons minced parsley
¼ cup chopped green bell pepper
2 tablespoons brown sugar
1 tablespoon chili powder
1 teaspoon salt
1 bay leaf
1 teaspoon monosodium glutamate
1 teaspoon oregano
¼ teaspoon celery seed
¼ teaspoon rosemary
¼ teaspoon thyme
¼ teaspoon marjoram
¼ teaspoon sweet basil
Juice of 1 lemon
1 cup sherry (optional)
3 scallions, chopped

Wash bean mixture. In a 3½-quart kettle, combine beans and water. Bring to a boil. Reduce heat and simmer, covered, for 1 hour. Add more water if necessary. Add all remaining ingredients except sherry. Bring to a slow boil and simmer, covered, until beans are tender, about 3 hours. Just before serving, remove bay leaf and stir in sherry. Garnish each serving with chopped scallions.

Serve with hot buttered tortillas or sourdough bread.

EDNA ST. VINCENT MILLAY SOUP

PREPARATION TIME: *1 hour, 30 minutes*
YIELD: *8 1-cup servings*

¾ **cup butter**

¼ **cup diced onion**

1½ **cups peeled and diced potatoes (about 2 small or 1 large)**

¼ **cup chopped celery**

¾ **cup diced carrots**

¾ **cup chopped broccoli**

¾ **cup cut green beans**

¾ **cup diced zucchini**

1 **small clove garlic**

1½ **teaspoons sugar**

Freshly ground pepper to taste

3 **cups chicken broth**

5 **chicken bouillon cubes**

1½ **cups water**

¾ **cup peas**

In large kettle, melt butter. Sauté onion 1-2 minutes. Reduce heat to low and add all remaining vegetables except peas. Cook until vegetables are tender, about 20-25 minutes. Add garlic, sugar, peppers, broth, bouillon cubes and water. Reduce heat and simmer, covered, 30 minutes. Add peas and simmer 10 minutes more.

This original recipe was made on a cold, wintry Wisconsin day when it was time to sit by a fire with a good novel or book of poetry. Hence, the name. It is also good on an afternoon of rain and chill during the Arizona winter.

> *"I will cook for my love a banquet of beets and cabbages,*
> *Leeks, potatoes, turnips, all such fruits . . .*
> *We will laugh like spring above the steaming, stolid winter roots."*
> *from "Thanksgiving Dinner" by Edna St. Vincent Millay.*

*Edna St. Vincent Millay, "Thanksgiving Dinner", Collected Lyrics of Edna St. Vincent Millay, Harper & Row, New York, 1969, pp. 234-235.

JADE AND IVORY SOUP

PREPARATION TIME: *25 minutes*
YIELD: *6-8 1-cup servings*

1	whole chicken breast
½	cup chicken broth
2	egg whites
1	tablespoon cornstarch
1	teaspoon salt
1	bunch spinach leaves
2	tablespoons oil
4	cups chicken broth
1	tablespoon sherry
2	tablespoons cornstarch dissolved in 2 tablespoons water

Skin, bone and purée chicken. In small bowl, soak chicken in ½ cup broth. In medium glass bowl, beat egg whites until stiff. Fold in 1 tablespoon cornstarch and salt. Steam spinach, squeeze out all moisture and chop very fine. Heat oil in wok or deep skillet. Stir-fry spinach for 10 seconds. Add remaining broth and sherry. Bring to boil. Stir in chicken mixture and return to boil. Stir in dissolved cornstarch to thicken.

LENTIL SOUP

PREPARATION TIME: *2 hours*
YIELD: *6 1-cup servings*

1	cup lentils
6	cups water
2	beef bouillon cubes
1	bay leaf
1	8-ounce can tomato sauce
1	medium onion, chopped
1	celery stalk, chopped
1	carrot, chopped
2	cloves garlic, minced
¼	cup olive oil
	Salt and pepper to taste
	Vinegar (optional)

Wash lentils. Simmer lentils, water and bouillon cubes for 1 hour. Add remaining ingredients except vinegar. Cook until vegetables are tender, about 30 minutes. Remove bay leaf. Salt and pepper to taste. Add 1 teaspoon vinegar to each bowl of soup when serving, if desired.

MINESTRONE SOUP

PREPARATION TIME: *3 hours*
YIELD: *8 1-cup servings*

½	pound Italian sausage, sliced crosswise
1	tablespoon oil
1	cup diced onion
1	clove garlic, minced
1	cup diced carrots
1	teaspoon basil
2	small zucchini, sliced
1	1-pound can Italian tomatoes, with liquid
2½	cups beef broth
2	cups finely shredded cabbage
	Salt and pepper to taste
1	1-pound can white kidney beans, with liquid
½	cup rice
½	cup red wine
	Parmesan cheese, grated
	Fresh parsley, chopped

Brown sausage in oil in deep saucepan or Dutch oven. Add onion, garlic, carrots and basil. Cook 5 minutes. Add zucchini, tomatoes with liquid, broth, cabbage, salt and pepper. Bring to a boil. Reduce heat and simmer, covered, 1 hour. Add beans with liquid, rice and wine. Cook until rice is tender, about 20 minutes. Cool and refrigerate. Twenty minutes before serving, reheat soup and check seasonings. Soup should be thick. Top with grated Parmesan and chopped parsley.

Serve with hot crusty Italian bread and a mixed green salad with Italian dressing.

PUMPKIN SOUP

PREPARATION TIME: *45 minutes*
YIELD: *8 1-cup servings*

2	tomatoes, peeled, seeded and chopped
1	medium onion, chopped
⅓	cup chopped green bell pepper
2	tablespoons oil
4	cups peeled, seeded and diced pumpkin
1¾	cups chicken broth
½	cup chopped turnip
½	cup chopped carrot
¼	teaspoon nutmeg
½	cup milk or light cream
	Salt and pepper to taste

In large saucepan, sauté tomatoes, onion and green bell pepper in oil until tender. Add pumpkin, broth, turnip, carrot and nutmeg. Simmer until pumpkin is tender, about 20 minutes. Purée in blender or food processor. May freeze at this point. Return mixture to saucepan. Add milk or cream. Heat thoroughly. Season to taste with salt and pepper.

Great use for that Halloween pumpkin! Canned pumpkin may be used.

POTATO LEEK SOUP

PREPARATION TIME: *1 hour*
YIELD: *6 1-cup servings*

3	leeks, thinly sliced
4	tablespoons butter
4	potatoes, peeled and thinly sliced
4	cups chicken broth
2	cups water
	Chives, chopped

Sauté leeks in butter until soft. Add potatoes. Mix well and sauté a few minutes to absorb butter. Add broth and water. Simmer 30-40 minutes. Purée in food processor or blender. Serve hot, cold, or at room temperature garnished with chives.

A great base for other hot or cold vegetable soups. During last 10 minutes of cooking, place 1 bunch spinach or 2 zucchini, sliced, or 1 bunch asparagus on top of potatoes to steam. Purée all together.

SAINT-GERMAIN PEA SOUP

PREPARATION TIME: *45 minutes*
YIELD: *6 1-cup servings*

1	**small head lettuce, shredded**
2	**cups green peas, fresh shelled or frozen**
1	**cup water**
1	**cup chopped leeks (green part only)**
2	**tablespoons butter**
2	**teaspoons chopped chervil**
1	**teaspoon sugar**
1	**teaspoon salt**
¼	**teaspoon pepper**
2	**cups chicken broth**
2	**cups heavy cream**

In saucepan, mix together lettuce, peas, water, leeks, butter, chervil, sugar, salt and pepper. Bring to a boil and cook until peas are tender. Set aside 3 tablespoons cooked peas for garnish. Purée remaining mixture in blender or food processor. Return to saucepan. Stir in broth. Just before serving, blend in cream and heat thoroughly. Garnish with reserved peas.

This soup from the Paris suburb Saint Germain is rich and very delicately flavored. For the calorie conscious, substitute light cream for heavy cream.

VEGETABLE STOCK

PREPARATION TIME: *1 hour*
YIELD: *approximately 1 quart*

Bits and pieces of fresh vegetables which are usually discarded:

carrot peelings

celery tops

cabbage cores

cauliflower stems

onion skins

mushroom stems

potato peelings

left-over, undressed salad

etc.

Put bits and pieces into saucepan. Cover with cold water. Let simmer for at least 20 minutes. Turn off heat and let sit until cool. Strain and refrigerate until needed.

May be used as a substitute for beef or chicken stock.

ZUCCHINI SOUP

PREPARATION TIME: *45 minutes*
YIELD: *6 1-cup servings*

1	**medium onion, grated**
½	**cup butter**
1½	**pounds zucchini, shredded**
½	**teaspoon nutmeg**
1	**teaspoon basil**
1	**teaspoon salt**
	Pepper to taste
1	**cup heavy cream (optional)**

In medium saucepan, sauté onion in butter until limp. Add zucchini and simmer, covered, 15 minutes. Add spices. Purée in blender or food processor. If desired, add cream. Can be served hot or cold.

COLD BUTTERMILK-RASPBERRY SOUP

PREPARATION TIME: *5 minutes plus chilling time*
YIELD: *4 1-cup servings*

½	**pint fresh raspberries**
1	**quart buttermilk**
⅓	**cup sugar**
2	**egg yolks**
1	**teaspoon lemon juice**
1	**cup heavy cream**

Reserve 4 raspberries for garnish. Pour remaining berries into bowl or tureen. With a fork, gently mash berries to release some of the juices. Stir in buttermilk, sugar, yolks and lemon juice. Whip cream. Reserve half for garnish and fold remaining whipped cream into soup. To serve, float a dollop of whipped cream in each serving. Place a raspberry on each dollop.

This recipe is from a Danish cooking school in Copenhagen.

COLD CUCUMBER SOUP

PREPARATION TIME: *35 minutes plus chilling time*
YIELD: *4-6 1-cup servings*

2	**tablespoons butter**
¼	**cup diced chopped onion**
2	**cups diced unpeeled cucumber**
1	**cup watercress leaves**
½	**cup diced raw potato**
2	**cups chicken broth**
½	**teaspoon salt**
¼	**teaspoon pepper**
¼	**teaspoon dry mustard**
1	**cup heavy cream**
2	**sprigs parsley, snipped**
2	**radishes, sliced**

In large saucepan, melt butter and sauté onion until transparent. Add cucumbers, watercress, potato, broth, salt, pepper and mustard. Bring to a boil. Simmer until potatoes are tender, about 15 minutes. Purée in blender or food processor. Chill. Before serving, add cream and garnish with snipped parsley and radish slices.

COLD CURRIED AVOCADO SOUP

PREPARATION TIME: *30 minutes plus chilling time*
YIELD: *10 1-cup servings*

8	very ripe avocados
⅔	cup lime juice
2	cloves garlic, crushed
2	tablespoons mayonnaise
1	teaspoon curry powder
2	cups heavy cream
2	cups chicken broth
¼	cup minced fresh parsley
2	tablespoons minced fresh coriander (or ½ teaspoon dried coriander)
1	teaspoon Tabasco sauce
	White pepper to taste

In blender or food processor, purée avocados, lime juice, garlic, mayonnaise, and curry powder until smooth. Transfer mixture to large bowl or tureen. Stir in cream, broth, parsley, coriander, Tabasco sauce and pepper. Cover with foil and chill for up to three days.

COLD MELON SOUP

PREPARATION TIME: *2½ hours plus chilling time*
YIELD: *6 1-cup servings*

1½	cups coarsely chopped cantaloupe
1½	cups coarsely chopped honeydew
2	cups fresh-squeezed orange juice (about 4 oranges)
⅓	cup fresh-squeezed lime juice
1½	cups finely chopped cantaloupe
1½	cups finely chopped honeydew
	Mint leaves (optional)

In blender or food processor, purée coarsely chopped melons with juices. Pour into serving bowl. Stir in finely chopped melons. Cover and chill several hours. Garnish each serving with mint leaves, if desired.

Simple but elegant summer soup.

COLD SOUR CHERRY SOUP

PREPARATION TIME: *45 minutes plus chilling time*
YIELD: *8 ½-cup servings*

3	cups cold water
1	cup sugar
1	cinnamon stick
4	cups pitted sour cherries (or canned sour cherries, drained)
1	tablespoon arrowroot
2	tablespoons cold water
¼	cup heavy cream
¾	cup red wine, chilled

In 2-quart saucepan, combine 3 cups cold water, sugar and cinnamon stick. Bring to a boil and add cherries. Partially cover and simmer 35-40 minutes if cherries are fresh, 10 minutes if canned. Remove cinnamon stick. Mix arrowroot and 2 tablespoons cold water into a paste. Beat paste into soup, stirring constantly. Bring soup almost to a boil. Reduce heat and simmer until clear and slightly thickened, about 2 minutes. Refrigerate until chilled. Before serving, stir in cream and wine. Serve in pre-chilled bowls.

CREAMED SOUP BASE

PREPARATION TIME: *20 minutes*
YIELD: *1¼ cups*

1½	cups chicken broth
4	tablespoons flour
2	tablespoons butter
1	tablespoon cream
1	egg yolk

In small saucepan, heat broth 10 minutes. Melt butter and stir in flour to make a roux. Whisk roux into broth. In small bowl, blend together cream and egg yolk. Gradually add ¼ cup of broth mixture. Pour contents of bowl into saucepan. Cook and stir for 10 minutes. Do not boil.

This is equivalent to 1 10½-ounce can cream of chicken soup.
Recipe may be doubled, but still use only 1 egg yolk.

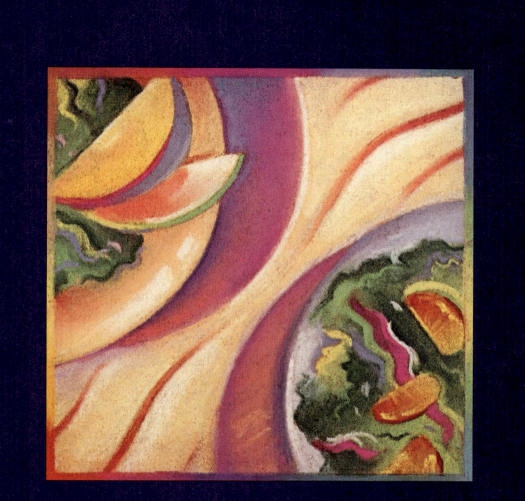

SALADS

Lighter Pleasures

ARTICHOKE, PIMENTO AND ONION TOSS

PREPARATION TIME: *10 minutes plus sitting time*
YIELD: *6-8 servings*

DRESSING
1	4-ounce jar pimentos, chopped
1	6-ounce jar marinated artichoke hearts, sliced
1	small Bermuda onion, thinly sliced
¼	cup olive oil
2	teaspoons sugar
⅓	cup red wine vinegar
1-2	cloves garlic, minced
¼	teaspoon freshly ground pepper
½	cup grated Parmesan cheese

Combine all dressing ingredients, including artichoke marinade. Mix and set aside for 30 minutes.

SALAD
1	head iceberg lettuce
1	head red leaf lettuce

To serve, tear greens into bite-size pieces. Pour dressing over greens and toss well.

BROCCOLI SALAD

PREPARATION TIME: *20 minutes plus chilling time*
YIELD: *4-6 servings*

DRESSING
1	cup mayonnaise
⅓	cup sugar
2	tablespoons red wine vinegar

Combine dressing ingredients. Refrigerate overnight to blend flavors.

SALAD
1	large bunch broccoli
1	cup dry roasted sunflower seeds
12	slices crisp bacon, crumbled
½	pint basket cherry tomatoes, halved
½	cup raisins (optional)

Using broccoli flowerettes only, combine with sunflower seeds, bacon, tomatoes and raisins. Toss with dressing.

CASHEW-PEA SALAD

PREPARATION TIME: *30 minutes*
YIELD: *6 servings*

DRESSING

⅓ **tablespoon lemon juice**

½ **cup red wine vinegar**

1½ **cups oil**

¾ **teaspoon salt**

½ **teaspoon freshly ground pepper**

2 **teaspoons Worcestershire sauce**

½ **teaspoon Dijon mustard**

1 **small clove garlic, minced**

½ **teaspoon sugar**

SALAD

1 **10-ounce package small frozen green peas, thawed**

1-2 **celery stalks, diced**

1-2 **scallions, diced**

1 **cup chopped cashews**

3-4 **slices crisp bacon, crumbled**

1 **cup sour cream**

Lettuce leaves

Tomato wedges

Mix together all dressing ingredients. Blend well and set aside.

Combine peas, celery, scallions, cashews, bacon and sour cream. Add ¼ cup of dressing to mixture and toss well.
To serve, spoon onto a bed of lettuce leaves and surround with tomato wedges.

CREAMY MARINATED POTATO SALAD

PREPARATION TIME: *40 minutes plus chilling time*
YIELD: *6 servings*

6	**medium red potatoes**
¼	**cup oil**
¼	**cup cider vinegar**
1	**medium onion, chopped**
1	**teaspoon salt**
¼	**teaspoon freshly ground pepper**
1	**teaspoon dill**
¾	**cup mayonnaise**
¼	**cup light cream**
3	**hard-cooked eggs, diced**
1-2	**celery stalks, thinly sliced**
	Lettuce leaves
1	**2-ounce jar pimentos, drained and chopped**

Boil potatoes until just done. Cool, peel and cut into thin slices. Place in large bowl and set aside.

Combine oil, vinegar, onion, salt, pepper and dill. Mix well. Pour over potatoes and toss gently. Cover and chill at least 3 hours.

To serve, blend mayonnaise with light cream. Pour over potatoes and toss to coat. Add eggs and celery. Toss lightly. Line salad bowl with lettuce leaves. Fill with salad and garnish with pimento.

CRISP DAY-BEFORE SLAW

PREPARATION TIME: *20 minutes plus chilling time*
YIELD: *8-10 servings*

8	**cups finely shredded cabbage (approximately 1 head)**
1	**small onion, chopped**
1	**medium green bell pepper, chopped**
12	**stuffed green olives, sliced**
⅓	**cup sugar**
½	**cup white vinegar**
½	**cup salad oil**
1	**teaspoon prepared mustard**
1	**teaspoon celery seed**

Combine cabbage, onion, green bell pepper and olives in a 9 x 13 inch glass casserole. Sprinkle with sugar. Mix vinegar, oil, mustard and celery seed. Pour over cabbage. Cover and refrigerate for 24 hours, tossing gently 2-3 times.

MARINATED MUSHROOMS

PREPARATION TIME: *25 minutes plus chilling time*
YIELD: *6-8 servings*

4	scallions, chopped
⅓	cup red wine vinegar
⅓	cup salad oil
1	teaspoon Worcestershire sauce
1	teaspoon prepared or dry mustard
1	teaspoon brown sugar
3	teaspoons snipped fresh parsley
1	teaspoon salt
¼	teaspoon freshly ground pepper
2	pounds fresh mushrooms, sliced
8	lettuce leaves
12	slices crisp bacon, crumbled

In small saucepan, combine scallions, vinegar, oil, Worcestershire sauce, mustard, sugar, parsley, salt and pepper. Heat to boiling. Add mushrooms and simmer 5-6 minutes. Let cool. Pour into glass bowl. Cover and refrigerate at least 4 hours. To serve, drain, arrange on lettuce leaves and garnish with bacon.

MIXED GREENS WITH STRAWBERRY DRESSING

PREPARATION TIME: *20 minutes*
YIELD: *6-8 servings*

DRESSING
½ **pint basket strawberries**

2 **tablespoons blueberry vinegar**

2 **tablespoons sugar**

¼ **cup olive oil**

1 **tablespoon strawberry jam**

Salt and pepper to taste

SALAD
8 **cups crisp salad greens, torn into bite-size pieces**

1 **small jicama, julienne cut**

1 **pint basket strawberries, halved**

2 **cups bean sprouts**

Purée strawberries with vinegar, sugar, oil and jam. Add salt and pepper to taste. Set aside.

To serve, combine greens, jicama, strawberries and sprouts. Pour dressing over salad and toss lightly.

OLD PUEBLO CLUB SALAD

PREPARATION TIME: *30 minutes*
YIELD: *8-10 servings*

DRESSING

1 cup oil

⅓ cup red wine vinegar

2 tablespoons anchovy paste

1 teaspoon salt

1 teaspoon freshly ground pepper

1 teaspoon oregano

½ teaspoon tarragon

1 teaspoon sugar

1 tablespoon Worcestershire sauce

Blend all dressing ingredients. Set aside.

SALAD

1 head iceberg lettuce

1 head romaine lettuce

½ head endive

2 ounces each: ham, turkey, salami, white and yellow cheese, julienne cut

½ cup garbanzo beans

Croutons

To serve, tear greens into bite-size pieces. Combine with ham, turkey, salami, cheeses and garbanzo beans. Glaze greens with dressing. Add croutons to absorb excess dressing. Toss well.

GARNISH

¼ cup grated Parmesan cheese

¼ cup shredded red cabbage

¼ cup shredded carrot

Sprigs of watercress

Garnish with Parmesan, cabbage, carrot and watercress.

The Old Pueblo Club, a private, well-established club of Tucson, is noted for its fine dining. This recipe has been adjusted from restaurant proportions to family-size.

ORANGE AND GREEN SALAD

PREPARATION TIME: *25 minutes*
YIELD: *6 servings*

DRESSING
- ½ teaspoon salt
- ⅛ teaspoon freshly ground pepper
- ¼ cup olive oil
- 2 tablespoons snipped fresh parsley
- 2 tablespoons sugar
- 2 tablespoons red wine vinegar
- 2-4 drops Tabasco sauce

GARNISH
- ½ cup slivered almonds
- 3 tablespoons sugar

SALAD
- 1 head iceberg lettuce
- 1 head romaine lettuce
- 2 celery stalks, thinly sliced
- 4 scallions, chopped
- 1 11-ounce can mandarin oranges, drained

Combine all dressing ingredients. Mix well. Cover and chill to allow flavors to blend while preparing remainder of ingredients.

In a dry skillet, over medium heat, toast almonds and sugar lightly until sugar just melts. Set aside.

To serve, tear greens into bite-size pieces and add celery, scallions and oranges. Pour dressing over greens. Toss well. Garnish with almonds.

CRANBERRY-BLUEBERRY MOLD

PREPARATION TIME: *15 minutes plus chilling time*
YIELD: *12 servings*

1 cup orange juice	
1 cup water	
2 3-ounce packages lemon gelatin	
¼ teaspoon salt	
1 cup orange juice	
1 16-ounce can whole cranberry sauce	
1 16-ounce can whole blueberries, drained (or ½ pint basket, fresh)	

Heat 1 cup orange juice and water to boiling. Pour over gelatin. Add salt. Stir in additional orange juice. Chill until partially set. Fold in cranberry sauce and blueberries. Pour into 5-cup mold. Chill at least 6 hours.

FROZEN FRUIT RING

PREPARATION TIME: *15 minutes plus chilling time*
YIELD: *12 servings*

2 cups sour cream	
2 tablespoons lemon juice	
¾ cup sugar	
⅛ teaspoon salt	
1 8-ounce can crushed pineapple, drained	
½ pint basket strawberries, diced	
2 small bananas, mashed	
½ cup chopped nuts	
Lettuce leaves	
Fresh mint leaves	

Mix sour cream, lemon juice, sugar and salt. Add pineapple, strawberries, bananas and nuts. Stir well. Pour into large ring mold and freeze. Allow to thaw 2-3 hours in refrigerator before serving. Place on bed of lettuce leaves. Garnish with mint.

SUMMER FRUIT SALAD

PREPARATION TIME: *30 minutes*
YIELD: *6-8 servings*

DRESSING

¾ **cup plain yogurt**

½ **cup sour cream**

3 **tablespoons honey**

½ **teaspoon orange zest**

¼ **teaspoon freshly ground nutmeg**

SALAD

1 **honeydew melon**

Lettuce leaves

4 **fresh peaches or nectarines**

Lemon juice

1 **cup fresh blueberries**

1 **cup fresh raspberries or strawberries**

Combine yogurt, sour cream, honey, orange zest and nutmeg. Blend well. Cover and chill.

Peel and slice melon into 6-8 1-inch thick rounds, discarding seeds. Place on individual plates on top of lettuce leaves. Peel and slice peaches. Coat with lemon juice and arrange on top of melon rounds. Sprinkle with berries. Pass chilled dressing to spoon over fruit.

ZESTY GAZPACHO MOLD

PREPARATION TIME: *30 minutes plus chilling time*
YIELD: *12 servings*

2	**envelopes unflavored gelatin**
1	**10-ounce can tomato-based chili sauce**
½	**cup water**
2	**medium tomatoes, very finely chopped**
1	**celery stalk, very finely chopped**
1	**medium cucumber, very finely chopped**
1	**small green bell pepper, very finely chopped**
1	**clove garlic, minced**
3	**scallions, finely chopped**
2	**tablespoons olive oil**
2	**tablespoons red wine vinegar**
1	**tablespoon lemon juice**
½	**teaspoon oregano**
½	**teaspoon chili powder**

In small saucepan, sprinkle gelatin over chili sauce and water. Let stand for 5 minutes to soften. Cook and stir over medium heat until gelatin is dissolved. Cool to room temperature. Add remaining ingredients. Stir. Pour into 4-cup mold. Cover and chill at least 4 hours.

CHRISTMAS-IN-JULY SALAD

PREPARATION TIME: *1 hour*
YIELD: *4 servings*

STRAWBERRY VINAIGRETTE

¼ **cup strawberry vinegar**

1 **tablespoon lime juice**

Salt and white pepper to taste

¾ **cup olive oil**

SALAD

¼ **pound snow peas**

¼ **honeydew melon**

1 **cup strawberries**

4 **large Boston lettuce leaves**

½ **pound ham, thinly sliced**

Combine all strawberry vinaigrette ingredients. Set aside.

Trim snow peas and remove strings. In a saucepan of salted boiling water, blanch snowpeas just until water returns to a boil. Drain in a colander and refresh peas under cold water. Cut into julienne strips. Remove rind from honeydew and cut into julienne strips. Rinse and hull strawberries and cut into julienne strips. In ceramic or glass bowl, combine snow peas, melon and strawberries. Toss with vinaigrette. In the center of each serving plate, place a mound of fruit mixture on a leaf of lettuce. Surround the lettuce with ham slices.

ANTIPASTO TOSS

PREPARATION TIME: *40 minutes*
YIELD: *10 servings*

DRESSING
1-2 cloves garlic, minced

1 tablespoon anchovy paste

3 tablespoons wine vinegar

¼ cup olive oil

SALAD
1 6-ounce jar marinated artichoke hearts

4 scallions, diced

1 small green bell pepper, julienne cut

1 cup cauliflower flowerettes

½ pint basket cherry tomatoes, halved

1 6-ounce can pitted ripe olives

1 2-ounce jar pimentos, chopped

1 cup garbanzo beans

½ teaspoon freshly ground pepper

1 1-pound package large pasta shells, cooked and drained

6 ounces salami, shredded

GARNISH
12 slices hard salami

Freshly grated Parmesan cheese

To prepare dressing, combine dressing ingredients with artichoke marinade. Blend well. Set aside.

In large bowl, combine all salad ingredients. Toss well.
To serve, add desired amount of dressing to salad mixture and toss lightly.

Arrange salami on top. Serve with Parmesan cheese.

CHICKEN-RICE SALAD WITH ARTICHOKES

PREPARATION TIME: *1 hour plus marinating time*
YIELD: *8-10 servings*

MARINADE

- ½ teaspoon celery seed
- 1 clove garlic, minced
- 1 scallion, finely chopped
- ¼ teaspoon sugar
- 1 tablespoon fresh snipped parsley
- ¼ cup red wine vinegar
- ⅓ cup olive oil
- 2 6-ounce jars marinated artichoke hearts, sliced
- 1 4-ounce jar pimentos, chopped
- 2 celery stalks, thinly sliced
- 1 small green bell pepper, chopped

In medium bowl, combine celery seed, garlic, scallions, sugar, parsley, vinegar and oil. Blend well. Add artichokes (including marinade), pimentos, celery and green bell pepper. Coat well and marinate overnight.

SALAD

- 2 6-ounce packages long grain and wild rice
- 4 whole chicken breasts, cooked and diced
- 1 cup mayonnaise
- 1 pound mushrooms, sliced
- 1 head iceberg lettuce

Using ½ cup less water for each package, cook rice according to package directions. Combine rice, chicken and mayonnaise. Add sliced mushrooms and marinated mixture. Stir and chill. Serve on lettuce cups.

CHINESE CHICKEN SALAD

PREPARATION TIME: *45 minutes plus chilling time*
YIELD: *6-8 servings*

DRESSING

4	**tablespoons sugar**
1	**teaspoon salt**
½	**teaspoon dry mustard**
4	**tablespoons red wine vinegar**
4	**tablespoons soy sauce**
3	**slices fresh ginger root**
2	**cloves garlic, slightly mashed**
½	**cup olive oil**

Combine all dressing ingredients in jar. Shake well and refrigerate overnight to blend flavors.

SALAD

2	**whole large chicken breasts, cooked**
1	**head iceberg lettuce**
3-4	**scallions, diagonally sliced**
4-5	**celery stalks, diagonally sliced**
½	**cup slivered almonds, toasted**
¼	**cup sesame seeds, toasted**

Dice chicken. Tear lettuce into bite-size pieces and add chicken, scallions, celery, almonds and sesame seeds. Remove ginger and garlic from dressing. Pour dressing over salad. Toss well.

LEMON-PISTACHIO BEEF SALAD

PREPARATION TIME: *20 minutes plus chilling time*
YIELD: *2 servings*

1 medium cucumber, thinly sliced

3 scallions, chopped

1 teaspoon salt

1 large lemon

1 teaspoon sugar

½ pound beef sirloin, cooked and cut in julienne strips

1 large carrot, shredded

1 celery stalk, thinly sliced

½ cup pistachios, shelled and chopped

1 large lemon, thinly sliced

Combine cucumber, scallions and salt. Cover and chill 30-60 minutes. Drain thoroughly and discard liquid. With vegetable peeler, remove all of the thin yellow outer peel from lemon. Cut peel into thin 1-inch slivers. Juice the remaining lemon. Mix 3 tablespoons of lemon juice with sugar and lemon peel. Pour mixture over cucumber and scallions. Add beef and mix together. Cover and chill for 2-6 hours, stirring occasionally. To serve, mix carrot, celery and pistachios with beef mixture. Mound salad on salad plates and arrange a border of halved lemon slices around each salad.

PASTA DEL SOL

PREPARATION TIME: *40 minutes plus chilling time*
YIELD: *6-8 servings*

DRESSING

½ cup orange juice
½ cup oil
1 tablespoon grated orange peel
1 tablespoon sugar
1 tablespoon crushed sweet basil
¼ teaspoon freshly ground pepper
⅛ teaspoon nutmeg

In small bowl, combine all dressing ingredients. Blend well. Set aside.

SALAD

1 20-ounce can chunk pineapple, drained
½ pound medium pasta shells, cooked
2 naval oranges, peeled and cut into cubes
1 red bell pepper, julienne cut
1-2 carrots, julienne cut
1 cup frozen peas, thawed
3-4 scallions, chopped
1 cup cashews

In large bowl, combine all salad ingredients. Pour dressing over salad. Toss well. Cover and refrigerate at least 4 hours or overnight.

For a creamier dressing, blend ⅓ cup sour cream, ⅓ cup mayonnaise and ¼ teaspoon snipped fresh dill. Add to drained salad right before serving.

ORIENTAL SHRIMP SALAD

PREPARATION TIME: *1 hour, 30 minutes*
YIELD: *6 servings*

DRESSING

1	**tablespoon dry mustard**
2	**tablespoons hot water**
½	**cup plum sauce**
3	**tablespoons rice vinegar**
2	**tablespoons sesame oil**
1	**tablespoon soy sauce**
1	**teaspoon salt**
1	**tablespoon sugar**

SALAD

1½	**pounds raw shrimp, shelled**
2	**tablespoons Chinese rice wine**
3	**slices fresh ginger peeled and slightly smashed**
¼	**teaspoon salt**
2	**ounces cellophane noodles**
8	**ounces fresh snow peas, strings removed**
1	**teaspoon sesame oil**
2	**tablespoons chicken broth**
2	**scallions, minced**

For dressing, whisk together dry mustard and hot water in small mixing bowl. Add remaining ingredients and whisk to combine.

Score shrimp along the length of the back and remove veins. Score deeply enough for shrimp to spread into a butterfly shape when cooked. Rinse shrimp, drain well and squeeze out excess moisture in kitchen towel. Combine rice wine, ginger and salt in large mixing bowl. Squeeze ginger slices with fingers repeatedly for about 2 minutes to release flavor. Add shrimp and toss to coat. Cover mixture and marinate at room temperature for 20 minutes. Remove and discard ginger. In large saucepan or wok, bring 1 quart water to boil. Add shrimp and simmer until just cooked through, about 1½ minutes. Drain and set aside.

Soften noodles in warm water to cover for 10 minutes. Drain well, cut with scissors into 3-inch lengths and reserve. Blanch snow peas in 1 quart boiling water in large saucepan or wok. Lift snow peas from water, reserving water. Rinse snow peas under cold running water. Drain and set aside. Bring reserved water back to boil and cook noodles for 1 minute. Rinse under cold running water, drain well and place in a bowl. Whisk together sesame oil and chicken broth. Pour over noodles. Toss lightly.

To serve, arrange noodles on platter and place snow peas on top. Arrange shrimp on snow peas and pour dressing over all. Sprinkle with minced scallions and toss lightly to coat all ingredients.

SALPICÓN

PREPARATION TIME: *3 hours*
YIELD: *8 servings*

2	**pounds flank steak**
2	**cups water**
¼	**small onion**
2-3	**garlic cloves**
¼	**teaspoon crushed oregano**
¼	**teaspoon crushed mint leaves**
1	**teaspoon salt**
3-4	**peppercorns**
3	**medium boiling potatoes**
3	**poblano chilies, roasted and peeled, or 3 whole canned green chilies, cut in thin strips**
½	**cup olive oil**
¼	**cup white vinegar**
1	**teaspoon Maggi seasoning**
	Salt and freshly ground pepper
¼	**cup olive oil (optional)**
2	**tablespoons vinegar (optional)**
10	**large romaine lettuce leaves**
1-2	**tablespoons olive oil**
2	**medium tomatoes, cut in wedges**
1	**medium Bermuda onion, sliced**
1	**small avocado, peeled and sliced**
	Strips of Queso Fresco, Monterey Jack or Swiss cheese

Place steak in a large saucepan. Add water, onion, garlic, oregano, mint, salt and peppercorns. Cover and simmer until meat is tender, about 1 hour, 45 minutes. Let cool. Drain and cut meat across grain into 2-inch long pieces. Use 2 forks to shred meat. Peel potatoes and cook in boiling salted water until tender, about 30 minutes. Drain; cool and cut into ½-inch cubes. In large bowl, combine meat, potatoes and chiles. Mix ½ cup olive oil, ¼ cup vinegar and Maggi seasoning. Add to meat mixture with salt and freshly ground pepper to taste. Toss gently. If more dressing is desired, add ¼ cup olive oil and 2 tablespoons vinegar. Wash lettuce leaves and slice crosswise into ½-inch pieces. Place lettuce on a large platter. Sprinkle lightly with 1-2 tablespoons olive oil. Arrange meat mixture on lettuce. Garnish with tomato wedges, onion slices, avocado slices and cheese strips.

SUMMER PASTA SALAD

PREPARATION TIME: *40 minutes*
YIELD: *6-8 servings*

DRESSING
¾	**cup mayonnaise**
1	**tablespoon tarragon vinegar**
1-2	**cloves garlic, finely minced**
1	**teaspoon salt**
½	**teaspoon freshly ground pepper**

In small bowl, combine all dressing ingredients. Mix well. Set aside.

SALAD
½	**pound spiral spinach noodles, cooked**
½	**pound spiral white noodles, cooked**
1	**tablespoon olive oil**
½	**pound fresh snow peas**
½	**pound cooked turkey breast, julienne cut**
1	**4-ounce jar pimentos, chopped**
2-3	**scallions, chopped**

Combine noodles with oil and coat well. Remove strings from snow peas. Cook in slightly salted boiling water for 2-3 minutes. Drain and rinse twice under cold water. Mix peas, turkey, pimentos and scallions with noodles. Add dressing and toss. Cover and chill.

Chicken, shrimp or crab meat may be substituted for turkey.

SOUTHWESTERN PASTA SALAD WITH CILANTRO PESTO

PREPARATION TIME: *2 hours*
YIELD: *10-12 servings*

PASTA
- 2 cups flour
- 2 tablespoons chili powder
- 3 eggs
- 1 tablespoon olive oil

SALAD
- 2 green bell peppers, thinly sliced
- 2 red bell peppers, thinly sliced
- 2 yellow bell peppers, thinly sliced
- 1 bunch scallions, sliced
- 3 tablespoons olive oil
- 2 pounds smoked turkey breast, thinly sliced

CILANTRO PESTO
- 2 cups cilantro
- 2 cloves garlic
- ½ cup walnuts
- 2 teaspoons salt
- ½ cup grated Parmesan cheese
- 1 cup olive oil

In a food processor, combine all pasta ingredients until dough forms pea-size pieces. Divide dough into 3 parts. Using one portion at a time, in a pasta machine, work dough to thinnest setting. Cut into noodles. Hang to dry.

Sauté peppers and scallions in hot oil. Add turkey and sauté 1 minute more. In large pot, cook pasta until just done. Drain well and toss with turkey mixture.

In food processor, chop cilantro, garlic and nuts. Add salt and Parmesan cheese and process into purée. Continue mixing and slowly drizzle in oil. Pour over pasta salad and toss.

This recipe is from The Tasting Spoon, adapted from a recipe by Alan Zeman, chef, Tucson Country Club.

TANGY SHRIMP WITH AVOCADO

PREPARATION TIME: *20 minutes plus chilling time*
YIELD: *6-8 servings*

DRESSING
- ¼ cup olive oil
- ¼ cup white wine vinegar
- 2 tablespoons lemon juice
- 2 cloves garlic, minced
- ½ teaspoon lemon pepper
- 3-4 scallions, chopped

SALAD
- 1 large avocado, peeled and diced
- 2 pounds shrimp, cooked and peeled
- 1 large head iceberg lettuce, shredded
- Cherry tomato halves

Combine all dressing ingredients. Stir and set aside.

Place avocado and shrimp in glass bowl and pour dressing over mixture. Gently turn to coat well. Cover and refrigerate for 1-2 hours. To serve, drain avocado and shrimp mixture, reserving dressing. Mound on lettuce and garnish with tomatoes. Pass dressing.

CREAMY MUSHROOM DRESSING

PREPARATION TIME: *15 minutes plus chilling time*
YIELD: *2½ cups*

- 1 cup mayonnaise
- 1 clove garlic, minced
- ¼ cup chopped chives
- ¼ cup snipped fresh parsley
- 1 tablespoon lemon juice
- 1 tablespoon white wine vinegar
- ½ teaspoon salt
- ½ teaspoon freshly ground pepper
- ½ cup sour cream
- ½ pound mushrooms, thinly sliced

Combine all ingredients except mushrooms. Blend well. Fold in mushrooms and chill 2-3 hours.

HOT BRIE DRESSING

PREPARATION TIME: *25 minutes*
YIELD: *2 cups*

10	ounces Brie cheese
½	cup olive oil
2	shallots, minced
2	cloves garlic, minced
½	cup sherry wine vinegar
2	tablespoons lemon juice
4	teaspoons Dijon mustard
	Freshly ground pepper

Cut Brie into small pieces and bring to room temperature. In large heavy skillet, warm oil over heat for 10 minutes. Add shallots and garlic. Cook until translucent, about 5 minutes. Stir in vinegar, lemon juice and mustard. Add cheese and stir until smooth. Season with pepper. Serve hot.

Especially good with salad made of endive, romaine and croutons.

ORANGE-MINT DRESSING

PREPARATION TIME: *20 minutes plus chilling time*
YIELD: *1½ cups*

⅓	cup orange juice
1	tablespoon sugar
2	teaspoons cornstarch
	Salt to taste
1	egg, lightly beaten
½	teaspoon grated orange peel
2	tablespoons lemon juice
⅓	cup sour cream
1	teaspoon finely chopped fresh mint (or ½ teaspoon dried)

Combine orange juice, sugar, cornstarch and salt in saucepan. Heat to boiling, stirring constantly. Remove from heat and cool slightly. Whisk in egg, orange peel and lemon juice. Fold in sour cream and mint. Cover and refrigerate until ready to use.

A distinctive-tasting dressing for fruits, fruit salads or cold poached chicken breasts.

ORANGE-GINGER VINAIGRETTE

PREPARATION TIME: *10 minutes*
YIELD: *1 cup*

1	**small shallot, minced**
1	**1-inch piece fresh ginger root, peeled and finely minced**
½	**teaspoon Dijon mustard**
¼	**teaspoon salt**
⅛	**teaspoon freshly ground white pepper**
3	**tablespoons white wine vinegar**
½	**cup oil**
½	**small orange, peeled, seeded and sectioned**

Combine all ingredients and blend well.

SAGE VINEGAR

PREPARATION TIME: *5 minutes plus steeping time*
YIELD: *2 cups*

2	**cups premium cider or wine vinegar**
½	**cup fresh sage leaves**

Two Week method: Pour vinegar into glass bottle or jar. Slightly bruise sage leaves and add to vinegar. Cap tightly and set in a sunny window for two weeks, turning frequently.

Overnight method: Heat vinegar (do not boil) and pour into glass bottle or ceramic crock. Add slightly bruised sage leaves; close tightly and steep overnight.

After steeping vinegar, using two-week or overnight method, strain and rebottle, adding a fresh sprig of sage for decoration.

RASPBERRY VINEGAR

PREPARATION TIME: *5 minutes plus 4-6 weeks standing time*
YIELD: *1½ cups*

1 cup French red wine vinegar (7% acidity*)	Pour vinegar and water in clean jar or decorative bottle. Add raspberries. Seal tightly and store in cool, dark place without shaking. Allow 4-6 weeks for flavor to develop. Once opened, store in cool, dark place and use within 3-4 months. Use in Raspberry Vinaigrette.
½ cup water	
7 fresh, cleaned red raspberries	

7% acidity vinegar is essential!
Other berries may be substituted for variation.

RASPBERRY VINAIGRETTE

PREPARATION TIME: *10 minutes plus chilling time*
YIELD: *1⅓ cups*

1 clove garlic	With mortar and pestle, press garlic and salt together. In small bowl, add garlic mixture to mustard. Stir in vinegar and mix well. Whisk in olive oil until well blended. Add pepper. Store in refrigerator.
½ teaspoon salt	
2 teaspoons Dijon mustard	
⅓ cup Raspberry Vinegar*	
1 cup olive oil	
¼ teaspoon freshly ground pepper	

See preceding recipe for Raspberry Vinegar.

SEAFOOD

Pleasures from the Waters

CURRIED SHRIMP AND SCALLOPS

PREPARATION TIME: *20-25 minutes*
YIELD: *4-6 servings*

2	tablespoons butter
1	onion, finely chopped
2	cloves garlic, minced
1-2	teaspoons Madras curry (or 2-3 teaspoons regular curry powder)
2	tablespoons butter
1	pound medium shrimp, peeled and cleaned
¾	pound scallops, rinsed
1	cup heavy cream
½	cup dry white wine
½	teaspoon savory
1	tablespoon cornstarch
2	tablespoons water
	Salt and pepper to taste

Serve over a bed of hot rice.

In large skillet, melt 2 tablespoons butter over medium heat. Add onion, garlic and curry. Sauté until onion is soft. Add remaining 2 tablespoons butter. Stir in shrimp and scallops. Cook until shrimp turn pink, about 3-5 minutes. With a slotted spoon, lift out seafood and set aside. Add cream, wine and savory to skillet. Dissolve cornstarch in water. Add to skillet. Cook, stirring until bubbly and thickened. Return seafood to skillet and heat through. Season to taste with salt and pepper.

SEAFOOD PASTA SUPREME

PREPARATION TIME: *45-60 minutes*
YIELD: *6 servings*

1	**8-ounce package vermicelli**
4	**tablespoons butter**
4	**tablespoons flour**
1	**cup chicken broth**
1	**cup heavy cream**
⅓	**cup shredded Gruyère or Swiss cheese**
2	**tablespoons sherry**
	White pepper to taste
¼	**pound mushrooms, quartered**
2	**tablespoons butter**
1½	**pounds cooked shrimp**
⅓	**cup grated Parmesan cheese**
½	**cup slivered almonds, toasted**

Cook and drain vermicelli. Melt 4 tablespoons butter in large saucepan. Blend in flour. Gradually add broth and cream. Cook over low heat, stirring constantly until sauce thickens. Blend in cheese, sherry and pepper. Stir until cheese melts. In small skillet, sauté mushrooms in 2 tablespoons butter and add to sauce. Remove from heat. Stir in shrimp and vermicelli. Transfer to casserole. Sprinkle with Parmesan cheese and almonds. Broil until lightly browned, about 6 minutes.

SUGGESTED WINE: Chateau Moncontour Vouvray

SESAME SHRIMP AND ASPARAGUS

PREPARATION TIME: *15 minutes*
YIELD: *6 servings*

1½	**pounds asparagus**
1	**tablespoon sesame seeds**
⅓	**cup oil**
2	**small onions, sliced**
1½	**pounds shrimp, peeled and cleaned**
4	**teaspoons soy sauce**
	Salt to taste

Trim asparagus and cut into 2-inch pieces. Set aside. In large skillet or wok, toast sesame seeds over medium heat until golden, stirring and shaking occasionally. Remove seeds and set aside. Add oil to skillet. Over medium heat, stir-fry asparagus, onions and shrimp until shrimp turn pink and vegetables are tender-crisp, about 5 minutes. Stir in seeds and soy sauce. Salt to taste.

Chinese pea pods may be substituted when asparagus is not in season.

SUGGESTED WINE: Clos du Bois Johannesburg Riesling

SHRIMP-ARTICHOKE CASSEROLE

PREPARATION TIME: *45 minutes*
YIELD: *4 servings*

4	tablespoons butter
4	tablespoons flour
¾	cup milk
¾	cup heavy cream
½	teaspoon salt
	Freshly ground pepper
1	20-ounce can artichokes, drained
1	pound shrimp, cleaned and cooked
¼	pound fresh mushrooms, sliced (about 1¼ cups)
2	tablespoons butter
¼	cup dry sherry
1	tablespoon Worcestershire sauce
¼	cup grated Parmesan cheese

In medium saucepan, melt 4 tablespoons butter. Whisk in flour until blended. Gradually beat in milk and cream. Stir until thickened and smooth. Season with salt and pepper. Set aside. In greased shallow baking dish, arrange artichokes, then shrimp. In small skillet, sauté mushrooms in remaining butter. Spoon over shrimp and artichokes. Sprinkle with sherry and Worcestershire sauce. Top with Parmesan cheese. Bake at 375 degrees until bubbly, about 20 minutes.

SUGGESTED WINE: Fetzer Chenin Blanc

SHRIMP CREOLE

PREPARATION TIME: *45 minutes*
YIELD: *4-6 servings*

1	clove garlic, chopped
½	cup chopped onion
⅓	cup chopped green bell pepper
4	tablespoons butter
1	2-pound can chopped tomatoes
1¾	cups water
¼	teaspoon pepper
¼	teaspoon dried rosemary
¼	teaspoon paprika
1	6-ounce package long grain and wild rice mix
1	pound shrimp, peeled and cleaned
	Salt to taste

In 3-quart saucepan, cook garlic, onion and green bell pepper in butter until tender, about 5 minutes. Add undrained tomatoes, water and seasonings. Stir in both packets from rice mix. Cover and simmer 20 minutes. Add shrimp. Cover and simmer until shrimp turn pink, about 10 minutes. Salt to taste.

SHRIMP WITH CURRY BUTTER BALLS

PREPARATION TIME: *30 minutes*
YIELD: *6 servings*

SHRIMP

2	pounds large shrimp, peeled and cleaned
½	pound lean bacon

Arrange shrimp on 6 skewers, lacing bacon strips in between. Set aside.

CURRY BUTTER BALLS

2	tablespoons butter
1	small onion, minced
2-3	teaspoons curry powder
1	tablespoon chopped chutney
¼	teaspoon white pepper
½	cup butter, softened
2	tablespoons freshly chopped parsley

In small skillet, melt 2 tablespoons butter. Sauté onion in butter until soft. Blend in curry powder and cook 2-3 minutes. Mix in chutney and let mixture cool slightly before blending in softened butter. Form into balls and chill well in refrigerator. Broil shrimp, turning once, until shrimp turn pink and bacon begins to crisp, about 5-7 minutes. Sprinkle with parsley and serve with curry butter balls.

SHRIMP WITH TARRAGON AND LEMON

PREPARATION TIME: *10-15 minutes*
YIELD: *6 servings*

2	pounds large shrimp, peeled and cleaned
½	cup butter
½	cup chicken broth
½	teaspoon dried tarragon
1	tablespoon chopped parsley
2	tablespoons lemon juice
2	teaspoons grated lemon zest
1	clove garlic, minced
2	tablespoons sherry

In large skillet, sauté shrimp in butter for 5 minutes. Add remaining ingredients, except sherry, and cook for another 5 minutes. Stir in sherry and serve immediately.

Serve over rice cooked with chicken broth and chopped scallions.

SUGGESTED WINE: Firestone Sauvignon Blanc

CRAB QUICHE

PREPARATION TIME: *1 hour, 30 minutes*
YIELD: *6 servings*

1	cup shredded Gruyère or Swiss cheese
1	unbaked 9-inch pie shell*
1	7½-ounce can crab meat, drained and flaked
3	scallions, sliced
3	eggs
1	cup light cream
½	teaspoon salt
½	teaspoon grated lemon zest
¼	teaspoon dry mustard
	Pinch of mace
¼	cup sliced almonds

Sprinkle cheese evenly over bottom of unbaked pie shell. Top with crab meat and scallions. In small bowl, beat eggs. Add cream, salt, lemon zest, dry mustard and mace. Pour over crab meat. Top with almonds. Bake at 325 degrees until set, about 45 minutes. Remove from oven and let stand for 10 minutes before serving.

*See recipe for Basic Pie Crust on page 196.

COLD LOBSTER WITH ARTICHOKES

PREPARATION TIME: *45-60 minutes*
YIELD: *4 servings*

2	1½-pound lobsters
½	pound green beans
3	cooked artichoke bottoms, thinly sliced
2	tablespoons tarragon vinegar
2	tablespoons lemon juice
2	teaspoons Dijon mustard
1	teaspoon salt
⅛	teaspoon red pepper (cayenne)
¼	cup olive oil
¼	cup salad oil
1	head butter lettuce
	Salt and pepper to taste

Drop lobsters, head first, into large pot of boiling salted water. Boil, covered, for 15 minutes. Drain and let cool. In small saucepan, cook beans for 8 minutes in enough boiling salted water to cover. Drain and rinse under cold water. Set aside. Remove meat from lobsters. Leaving claw meat whole, cut tail into ¼-inch slices. In small bowl, combine meat with artichoke bottoms. In another bowl, combine vinegar, lemon juice, mustard, 1 teaspoon salt and red pepper. Add olive oil and salad oil in a stream, beating constantly. Shred the inner leaves of lettuce and divide among 4 chilled plates. Toss lobster mixture with ¼ cup dressing, or enough to mix well. Add salt and pepper to taste. Divide lobster mixture among the plates and garnish each with green beans. Serve remaining dressing separately.

May be prepared ahead of time and put on chilled plates at the last minute. A very showy dish!

SUGGESTED WINE: Jordan Chardonnay

72

SEAFOOD PUFF

PREPARATION TIME: *1 hour, 10 minutes*
YIELD: *4 servings*

8	slices white bread, crusts removed
¾	cup cooked crab meat
¾	cup cooked shrimp
½	cup minced celery
3	tablespoons minced scallions
2	tablespoons parsley
4	tablespoons mayonnaise
1	tablespoon lemon juice
1	teaspoon Dijon mustard
4	slices processed American or Swiss cheese
2	eggs
1	cup milk

Arrange four slices of bread in greased 8-inch square casserole. In bowl, combine crab, shrimp, celery, scallions, parsley, mayonnaise, lemon juice and mustard. Spread mixture over bread. Arrange remaining four slices of bread on top. Place slice of cheese on each piece of bread. Beat eggs and milk together and pour over all. Cover and bake at 325 degrees for 35-40 minutes. Uncover and bake 10 minutes more. This is when it puffs!

SUGGESTED WINE: Chateau St. Jean Brut Champagne

TROUT WITH CAPER SAUCE

PREPARATION TIME: *30-45 minutes*
YIELD: *6 servings*

3	tablespoons butter
3	tablespoons flour
¾	cup hot beer
½	teaspoon salt
½	cup capers
1	tablespoon chopped parsley
	Juice of 1 lime
6	1-pound pieces rainbow or brook trout

In saucepan, melt butter. Stir in flour. Gradually whisk in ¾ cup hot water and beer, stirring until sauce is thick and smooth. Add remaining ingredients and keep warm. Split fish and grill until flakey, about 10-12 minutes. Serve hot with sauce.

A terrific summer dinner, served with roasted, sweet corn-on-the-cob and cold beer.

SUGGESTED WINE: Jekel Pinot Blanc

BAY SCALLOPS WITH VODKA AND CRÈME FRAÎCHE

PREPARATION TIME: *20 minutes plus chilling time*
YIELD: *4 servings*

1	pound bay scallops, rinsed
3-4	tablespoons vodka
1-2	teaspoons grated lemon zest
2	tablespoons chopped fresh dill (or ½ tablespoon dried)
¾	cup Crème Fraîche*
	Paprika

In small bowl, toss scallops with vodka, zest and dill. Place scallops in single layer in individual scallop shells. Spoon Crème Fraîche over scallops and sprinkle lightly with paprika. Cover and refrigerate at least 3 hours, but not longer than 24 hours. Broil scallops 6 inches from heat until top is well browned and scallops are just tender, about 4-5 minutes.

Looks so impressive, but it's so simple!
*Crème Fraîche recipe follows.

CRÈME FRAÎCHE

PREPARATION TIME: *5 minutes plus sitting time*
YIELD: *1 cup*

1	cup heavy cream
2	tablespoons buttermilk

Heat cream and buttermilk until just warm. Pour into glass jar and cover with plastic wrap. Let sit at room temperature for 24-36 hours, until almost as thick as sour cream. Seal tightly and refrigerate. Will keep for 2-3 weeks.

SCALLOPS DIJONNAISE

PREPARATION TIME: *50 minutes plus marinating time*
YIELD: *4-6 servings*

2	**pounds scallops, rinsed**
3	**tablespoons lemon juice**
3	**tablespoons dry white wine**
2	**whole eggs**
2	**egg yolks**
	Flour
2	**cloves garlic, minced**
½	**cup butter**
1	**cup dry white wine**
1	**cup chopped scallions**
1	**cup heavy cream**
½	**cup Dijon mustard**
	Salt and pepper to taste
2	**tablespoons freshly chopped parsley**

In small bowl, marinate scallops in lemon juice and white wine, covered, for 1 hour. Drain scallops and pat dry with paper towels. Beat whole eggs together with egg yolks. Dredge scallops in flour seasoned with salt and pepper and dip them in beaten eggs. In large skillet, sauté garlic in butter over moderate heat for 1 minute. Add scallops and sauté until golden brown. Transfer to heated platter. Add remaining wine to skillet and deglaze it over high heat. Add scallions, cream, mustard and salt and pepper to taste. Cook until sauce is reduced and thickened. Pour sauce over scallops and garnish with chopped parsley.

SCALLOPS IN MUSHROOM SAUCE

PREPARATION TIME: *30 minutes plus marinating time*
YIELD: *2-3 servings*

1	**pound bay scallops**
¼	**cup dry white wine**
1	**tablespoon chopped parsley**
1	**onion, chopped**
3	**tablespoons butter**
½	**teaspoon sweet paprika**
	Pinch of cumin
	Pinch of basil
6	**mushrooms, sliced**
2	**strips pimento, chopped**
1	**cup Béchamel Sauce***
	Salt to taste
	White pepper to taste
2	**tablespoons grated Romano cheese**

In glass bowl, combine scallops, wine and parsley. Cover and marinate in refrigerator for 1 hour. In skillet, cook onion in butter over medium heat, stirring, until golden. Add spices, mushrooms and pimentos. Cook and stir for 5 minutes. Add Béchamel Sauce and cook over low heat for another 5 minutes. Drain scallops. Add to sauce and simmer until scallops are tender, about 3-5 minutes. Season with salt and white pepper to taste. Divide among heated serving bowls and sprinkle with Romano cheese.

Béchamel Sauce recipe follows.

BÉCHAMEL SAUCE

PREPARATION TIME: *30 minutes*
YIELD: *2¼ cups*

1	**tablespoon minced onion**
3	**tablespoons butter**
4	**tablespoons flour**
3	**cups milk, scalded**
¼	**teaspoon salt**
	White pepper to taste

In saucepan, cook onion in butter until softened. Stir in flour and cook roux over low heat, stirring, for 3 minutes. Remove pan from heat. Add milk and whisk mixture until thick and smooth. Add salt and pepper to taste and simmer for 15 minutes. Strain through a fine sieve into a bowl and cover with buttered round of wax paper.

TERIYAKI SCALLOPS

PREPARATION TIME: *30 minutes plus marinating time*
YIELD: *4-6 servings*

1	pound large scallops, rinsed
¼	cup soy sauce
¼	cup dry sherry or sake
2	tablespoons sugar
2	tablespoons oil
¾	teaspoon ginger
1	clove garlic, minced

Cut scallops in half and place in small bowl. Combine remaining ingredients and pour over scallops. Marinate 30 minutes at room temperature. Drain scallops, reserving marinade. Thread scallops on 4-6 skewers. Place in greased, shallow baking pan. Bake at 450 degrees for 15 minutes, turning and basting several times with marinade.

Serve with fluffy white rice and stir-fry vegetables.

SUGGESTED WINE: Konocti Cabernet Blanc

FILLET OF SOLE DIJON

PREPARATION TIME: *20-30 minutes*
YIELD: *8 servings*

½	cup butter
½	cup white wine vinegar
1	tablespoon Dijon mustard
2	teaspoons salt
2	teaspoons lemon juice
1	teaspoon savory
½	teaspoon pepper
1	clove garlic, crushed
1-2	drops Tabasco sauce
8	fillets of sole
	Salt and pepper to taste

In small saucepan, combine all ingredients, except fillets. Simmer on low heat for 5 minutes. Place fillets in shallow baking dish. Season with salt and pepper. Pour sauce on top. Broil until fillets flake with a fork, about 10 minutes.

SUGGESTED WINE: Concannon Chardonnay

FISH FILLETS IN FOIL

PREPARATION TIME: *45 minutes*
YIELD: *4 servings*

⅓ cup orange juice

2 tablespoons malt vinegar

1 tablespoon soy sauce

4 fish fillets (sole, flounder or orange roughie)

1 cup chopped broccoli

1 cup sliced carrots

1 celery stalk cut into 1-inch pieces

½ orange, sliced

In small bowl, mix orange juice, vinegar and soy sauce. Set aside. Place each fillet in the center of a separate 12-inch square of foil. Arrange vegetables on each fillet. Pour sauce over each. Fold foil over each fillet, securing seams tightly. Place on cookie sheet. Bake at 450 degrees for 30 minutes. With a spatula, transfer individual servings to heated plates. Spoon a small amount of sauce over each. Garnish with orange slices.

Easy, low calorie dinner!

GRILLED SALMON DIABLE

PREPARATION TIME: *45 minutes*
YIELD: *6 servings*

---

6 large 1-inch thick salmon steaks

⅓ cup butter, softened

2 tablespoons lemon juice

2 teaspoons Dijon mustard

⅛ teaspoon red pepper (cayenne)

1 tablespoon minced parsley

Olive oil

Liquid Smoke

Soak salmon in 1 quart salted water for 30 minutes. While salmon is soaking, beat butter until creamy. Gradually beat in lemon juice until mixture is fluffy. Beat in mustard, red pepper and parsley. Set aside. Brush salmon with olive oil and liquid smoke. Grill 6 inches above hot coals. Turn once with wide spatula. Cook until fillets flake in center, about 10 minutes. Top each fillet with an equal portion of butter mixture.

Serve with Creamy Marinated Potato Salad, page 42, for a special summertime cookout.

HALIBUT ALYEOKA

PREPARATION TIME: *45 minutes*
YIELD: *6 servings*

1½	**pounds halibut or other white fish**
1	**clove garlic, mashed**
½	**teaspoon salt**
	Pepper to taste
	Juice of 1 lemon
1¼	**cups sour cream**
¾	**cup mayonnaise**
¾	**cup finely chopped onion**
¼	**cup chopped parsley**
¾-1	**cup grated Cheddar cheese**

Season fish on both sides with garlic, salt and pepper. Place in greased baking dish. Sprinkle with lemon juice. In small bowl, mix sour cream, mayonnaise, onions and parsley. Spread over top of fish. Top with grated cheese. Bake at 350 degrees until fish flakes with a fork, about 25 minutes. Don't overcook!

MAHI MAHI WITH MACADAMIA NUTS

PREPARATION TIME: *25 minutes plus marinating time*
YIELD: *4 servings*

1½	**pounds fresh or frozen mahi mahi fillets**
1	**8¾-ounce can pineapple slices**
1	**tablespoon soy sauce**
¼	**teaspoon salt**
	Pepper to taste
½	**teaspoon ginger**
¼	**cup chopped macadamia nuts**

Remove skin and cut fillets into 4 portions. Drain pineapple and reserve ½ cup syrup. In small bowl, combine reserved syrup with soy sauce, salt and pepper. Place fish in single layer in shallow dish. Pour syrup mixture over fish and let stand at room temperature for 30 minutes, turning once. Drain and reserve marinade. Place fish on greased broiler rack. Broil 4 inches from heat, until fillets flake easily with fork, about 10 minutes. Brush often with reserved marinade. During last few minutes of broiling, place pineapple slices on fillets. Brush with marinade and heat through. Sprinkle nuts on fish and pineapple slices.

SOLE WITH BASIL AND TOMATOES

PREPARATION TIME: *1 hour*
YIELD: *2-4 servings*

2	tablespoons butter
2	tablespoons flour
½	cup sherry
½	cup chicken broth
2	teaspooons fresh basil (or ½ teaspoon dried)
½	teaspoon thyme
2	tablespoons chopped chives
	Salt and pepper to taste
2	pounds fillet of sole
3	tomatoes, peeled and sliced

In saucepan, melt butter and stir in flour. Gradually whisk in sherry and broth. Add herbs. Stir and cook until thickened. Set aside. Salt and pepper fillets and place in a greased casserole. Place tomato slices on top. Pour sauce over all. Bake at 300 degrees for 30 minutes.

SUGGESTED WINE: Beaujolais Villages Vercherre

TARRAGON BUTTER

PREPARATION TIME: *10 minutes*
YIELD: *½ cup*

2-3	drops tarragon vinegar
	Salt to taste
	Freshly ground pepper to taste
3	tablespoons finely cut fresh tarragon leaves
7	tablespoons butter, cut in pieces

Add vinegar, salt and pepper to tarragon leaves and put through finest disk of a food mill. Add butter through disk. Work into smooth paste with wooden spatula. Refrigerate.

This versatile topping freezes well.

BROWN SUGAR SAUCE

PREPARATION TIME: *15 minutes*
YIELD: *1½ cups*

½ cup brown sugar

2 teaspoons Worcestershire sauce

2 teaspoons soy sauce

½ cup butter

1 small clove garlic, mashed

2 teaspoons dry mustard

¼ cup lemon juice

Mix all ingredients together in small saucepan. Simmer until smooth.

An unusual sauce for fish or duck.

DILL SAUCE

PREPARATION TIME: *45 minutes*
YIELD: *4 cups*

2 tablespoons shortening

2 tablespoons butter

1 cup chopped and firmly packed fresh young dill weed

1 teaspoon sugar

Salt to taste

2 cups chicken broth

2-3 tablespoons flour

1 cup milk

½ cup light cream

4 tablespoons vinegar

Juice of ½ lemon

¼ teaspoon white pepper

½ cup light cream

1 cup sour cream

In large saucepan, melt shortening and butter over medium heat. Add dill, sugar and salt. Stir until thoroughly heated. Add chicken broth and bring to a boil. Mix flour with milk and ½ cup light cream. Pour mixture into boiling liquid, stirring constantly with whisk. Reduce heat. Add vinegar, lemon juice and white pepper. Simmer for at least 20 minutes, stirring occasionally. In small bowl, mix remaining ½ cup light cream with sour cream. Slowly spoon some of the hot sauce into cream mixture to warm it. Then add to rest of hot sauce. Cover. Keep warm for 5 minutes before serving.

This delicate sauce is delicious with fish.

POULTRY

Savory Pleasures

BROILED TARRAGON CHICKEN BREASTS

PREPARATION TIME: *1 hour*
YIELD: *12 servings*

1 shallot, peeled

2 cloves garlic, peeled

¼ cup parsley, firmly packed

12 tablespoons unsalted butter

3 tablespoons tarragon

Salt and white pepper to taste

12 half chicken breasts, skin intact

Mince together shallot, garlic and parsley. Add butter, tarragon, salt and pepper. Purée mixture. Loosen skin on each breast with fingers, making a pocket without tearing the skin. Place 1 tablespoon herb mixture in each pocket. Spread by pressing on outside of skin. Place chicken, skin side down, on rack in broiling pan. Salt and pepper rib side of breasts. Broil 7-9 inches from heat until browned, about 15 minutes. Turn chicken and season skin lightly with salt and pepper. Broil until brown and tender, about 20 minutes.

CHEESE-STUFFED CHICKEN BREASTS

PREPARATION TIME: *1 hour plus chilling time*
YIELD: *6 servings*

12	ounces cream cheese, softened
⅓	cup blue cheese
5	tablespoons butter, softened
1	teaspoon freshly grated nutmeg
¾	cup grated Swiss cheese
6	half chicken breasts
3	teaspoons Dijon mustard
⅓	cup flour
1	egg, beaten
¼	cup bread crumbs
4	tablespoons butter

Blend together cream cheese, blue cheese, butter and nutmeg. Shape cheese into 6 ovals. Roll ovals in Swiss cheese and chill 1 hour. Skin, bone and flatten chicken breasts to ¼-inch thickness. Spread each breast with 1/2 teaspoon mustard. Place 1 cheese oval on each chicken breast. Fold chicken around cheese, enclosing oval like an envelope. Secure with toothpick if needed. In 3 separate bowls, place flour, egg and bread crumbs. Roll each chicken breast in flour, then egg, then bread crumbs. Chill for 1 hour. In heavy oven-proof skillet, sauté chicken in butter over high heat for 2-3 minutes until lightly browned on all sides. Transfer skillet to preheated oven and bake at 400 degrees for 7-10 minutes.

SUGGESTED WINE: Chateau Bouchaine Pinot Noir

CHICKEN WITH CRAB SAUCE

PREPARATION TIME: *1 hour plus marinating time*
YIELD: *8 servings*

CHICKEN

8	half chicken breasts
½	teaspoon Beau Monde
½	teaspoon salt
½	teaspoon lemon pepper
¾	cup white wine

SAUCE

½	pound mushrooms, sliced
1	scallion, sliced
2	tablespoons butter
5	cups Creamed Soup Base*
½	cup light cream
½	cup white wine
½	teaspoon Beau Monde
1	pound Alaskan King crab meat

See recipe for Creamed Soup Base on page 37.

Rub chicken with mixture of Beau Monde, salt and lemon pepper. Place in 9 x 13-inch glass dish. Cover with wine and marinate overnight. Remove chicken and reserve marinade. Bake at 350 degrees until tender, about 1 hour. Baste frequently with marinade. While chicken is baking, prepare sauce.

In a large skillet or heavy saucepan, sauté mushrooms and scallion in butter for 2 minutes. Stir in soup base, cream, wine and Beau Monde. Heat thoroughly. Add cooked crab, reserving a few large pieces for garnish. Serve sauce over chicken.

CHICKEN DIJON IN PHYLLO

PREPARATION TIME: *1 hour*
YIELD: *6 servings*

3	whole chicken breasts
½	teaspoon salt
¼	teaspoon white pepper
4	tablespoons butter
½	cup Dijon mustard
2	cups heavy cream
8	phyllo pastry sheets
12	tablespoons butter, melted
¼	cup bread crumbs
1	egg
1	teaspoon water

Skin, bone and cut chicken into 1-inch strips. Sprinkle with salt and pepper. Sauté in 4 tablespoons butter until strips are no longer pink, about 5 minutes. Transfer to platter and keep warm. Add mustard to skillet, scraping pan. Whisk in cream, blending thoroughly. Reduce heat and simmer until sauce is slightly thickened and reduced. Stir in any juices from chicken. Strain sauce over chicken. Lay 1 sheet of phyllo on a damp dish towel. Brush liberally with melted butter and sprinkle with 1-2 pinches of bread crumbs. Layer 6 more sheets of phyllo on top, preparing each with butter and bread crumbs. Top with last sheet of phyllo, brushing only the borders with melted butter. Arrange chicken over lower third of long side of dough, leaving a 2-inch border along outside edges. Turn up bottom edge, then fold in side edges, partially enclosing chicken. Roll up jelly-roll fashion. Place seam side down on lightly greased baking sheet. Beat egg with water and brush over dough to glaze. Bake at 450 degrees until phyllo is crisp and golden brown, about 12-15 minutes. Cut into 2-inch slices.

SUGGESTED WINE: River Oaks Chardonnay

CHICKEN FRICASSÉE WITH DUMPLINGS

PREPARATION TIME: *2 hours*
YIELD: *6 servings*

CHICKEN

1	4½-5½-pound chicken
½	teaspoon salt
½	teaspoon pepper
4	tablespoons butter
2	tablespoons oil
1	onion stuck with 2 cloves
1	carrot, halved
	Bouquet garni: 3 sprigs parsley, 2 celery tops, 1 bay leaf
7	cups chicken broth

SAUCE

4	tablespoons butter
⅓	cup flour
½	cup heavy cream
	Salt and pepper to taste

DUMPLINGS

2	cups flour
4	teaspoons baking powder
1½	teaspoons salt
¼	cup shortening
⅔	cup milk
¼	cup minced parsley
2	eggs, slightly beaten

Cut chicken into serving pieces. Dry and sprinkle with salt and pepper. Sauté chicken in 4 tablespoons butter and oil until well browned on all sides. Transfer chicken to large pot and add prepared onion, carrot, bouquet garni and chicken broth. Bring to a boil. Skim froth. Reduce heat and simmer, covered, until almost tender, about 1 hour. Transfer chicken to platter and keep warm. Reserve 7 cups broth, skimmed and strained.

In large covered flame-proof casserole, melt 4 tablespoons butter and stir in flour. Cook roux over low heat, stirring constantly, for 3 minutes. Remove from heat. Add reserved broth in a steady stream, stirring constantly. Bring mixture to a boil, reduce heat and simmer 10 minutes. Add cream. Salt and pepper to taste. Add chicken and bring to a boil. Into medium bowl sift together flour, baking powder and salt. Blend in shortening until mixture resembles corn meal. Add milk, parsley and eggs, stirring only until flour is moistened. Drop dumplings by tablespoons into chicken casserole and steam, covered, for 12 minutes.

SUGGESTED WINE: Fetzer Gamay Beaujolais

CHICKEN GARAM MASALA

PREPARATION TIME: *45 minutes*
YIELD: *4-6 servings*

½ teaspoon saffron threads

2 tablespoons oil

½ onion, chopped

½ green bell pepper, chopped

1 tablespoon water

½ teaspoon coriander

½ teaspoon red pepper (cayenne)

½ teaspoon salt

1½ cups finely chopped fresh tomatoes (about 2 large tomatoes)

½ cup plain yogurt

½ teaspoon garam masala

3 cups cooked and shredded chicken (about 1 whole chicken)

¾ cup water

¼ cup lemon juice

½ cup plain yogurt

Sprinkle saffron threads into small, dry skillet and toast for 30 seconds over low heat, shaking constantly. Transfer threads to small bowl. When cool to touch, crumble with fingers. Heat oil in deep skillet. Add onions, green bell pepper, 1 tablespoon water, coriander, red pepper and salt. Sauté until onions are soft and golden, about 8-10 minutes. Add small amount additional water if necessary. Add tomatoes, yogurt and a pinch of garam masala. Stir constantly for 2 minutes over low heat. Add saffron threads and chicken. Gradually add ¾ cup water and lemon juice. Bring mixture to a boil. Sprinkle in remainder of garam masala. Reduce to low heat. Cover and simmer 30 minutes. Before serving, stir in remaining ½ cup yogurt.

Curry powder may be substituted for garam masala.

CHEESE-GLAZED CHICKEN

PREPARATION TIME: *1 hour*
YIELD: *10-12 servings*

8	**whole chicken breasts**
2	**tablespoons flour**
1	**teaspoon salt**
1	**teaspoon pepper**
2	**tablespoons butter**
1	**tablespoon oil**
¼	**cup sherry**
1	**teaspoon cornstarch**
¾	**cup light cream**
½	**teaspoon salt**
⅓	**cup white wine**
1	**tablespoon lemon juice**
½	**cup grated Swiss cheese**
1	**teaspoon paprika**

Skin and bone chicken breasts. Combine flour, 1 teaspoon salt and pepper in bag. Place chicken in bag and shake until coated. In large skillet, brown chicken in butter and oil for about 5 minutes on each side. Add sherry. Cover and simmer over low heat until tender, about 25 minutes. Remove chicken to covered oven-proof serving dish. In small bowl, blend cornstarch, cream and ½ teaspoon salt. Stir mixture into pan drippings and continue cooking until sauce thickens. Add wine and lemon juice. Pour sauce over chicken. Sprinkle with cheese. Cover and let stand 15 minutes. Place chicken under broiler to brown and glaze top. Dust with paprika.

BAKED CHICKEN SUPREME

PREPARATION TIME: *1 hour, 45 minutes*
YIELD: *6 servings*

6	**half chicken breasts**
½	**cup flour**
½	**teaspoon salt**
¼	**teaspoon pepper**
½	**teaspoon paprika**
4	**slices bacon**
½	**cup chopped celery**
1	**pound mushrooms, sliced**
1	**small onion, chopped**
1	**teaspoon Worcestershire sauce**
½	**cup sherry**

Shake chicken in bag with flour, salt, pepper and paprika. In 2-quart casserole place chicken in single layer, skin side down. Bake at 400 degrees for 1 hour, turning once. While chicken is baking, fry bacon. Drain and crumble. In bacon fat, sauté celery until tender. Add mushrooms, onion, Worcestershire sauce and sherry. Cook 5 minutes longer. Pour mixture over chicken. Sprinkle bacon over top. Cover casserole and bake at 350 degrees for 30 minutes.

CHICKEN JUBILEE

PREPARATION TIME: *1 hour, 30 minutes*
YIELD: *10-12 servings*

4	chicken fryers, quartered
	Salt and pepper to taste
½	cup butter, melted
1	16-ounce can Bing cherries
½	cup golden raisins
½	cup brown sugar
1	clove garlic, crushed
2	onions, sliced
1	12-ounce bottle chili sauce
1	tablespoon Worcestershire sauce
1	cup sherry

Place chicken in shallow roasting pan, skin side up. Season and dribble with butter. Broil under medium heat until brown. Drain cherry liquid into measuring cup. Reserve cherries. Add enough water to liquid to measure 1 cup. Pour liquid into small bowl and add raisins, sugar, garlic, onions, chili sauce and Worcestershire sauce. Mix thoroughly. Pour sauce over chicken and cover. Bake at 325 degrees for 45 minutes. Add sherry and reserved cherries. Bake, uncovered, 15 minutes longer.

Mandarin oranges add a nice touch of color.
Plum jelly can be used to thicken sauce before final 15 minutes of roasting.

CHICKEN-PECAN CUTLETS

PREPARATION TIME: *25 minutes*
YIELD: *4 servings*

4	**half chicken breasts**
1	**cup finely chopped pecans**
2	**ounces Provolone cheese, shredded**
½	**cup dried bread crumbs**
1	**teaspoon sage**
	Salt and pepper to taste
1	**egg**
2	**tablespoons water**
4	**tablespoons butter**
1	**tablespoon oil**

Skin, bone and flatten chicken to ¼-inch thickness. On a dinner plate combine nuts, cheese, bread crumbs, sage, salt and pepper. In small bowl beat egg and water. Coat each cutlet with nut mixture, then dip in egg, then nut mixture again. In large skillet, heat butter and oil together. Sauté each cutlet just until done, about 2-3 minutes on each side.

SUGGESTED WINE: Teduta Chianti Classico

CHICKEN RATATOUILLE

PREPARATION TIME: *30 minutes*
YIELD: *4 servings*

¼ cup oil

6 half chicken breasts, boned and cubed

2 zucchini, sliced

1 eggplant, peeled and cubed

1 large onion, sliced

1 green bell pepper, chopped

½ pound mushrooms, sliced

1 16-ounce can tomatoes, cut into large pieces

1 clove garlic, minced

1 teaspoon basil

1 teaspoon dried parsley

Salt and pepper to taste

In large skillet, heat oil. Sauté chicken about 2 minutes on each side. Add zucchini, eggplant, onion, green bell pepper and mushrooms. Cook until vegetables are tender-crisp, about 15 minutes. Add tomatoes, stirring carefully. Add garlic, basil, parsley, salt and pepper. Simmer 5 minutes or until chicken is fork tender.

Arrange on platter around a bed of rice.

CHICKEN WITH LOBSTER

PREPARATION TIME: *40 minutes*
YIELD: *8-10 servings*

12	half chicken breasts, boned
4	tablespoons butter
1½	pounds mushrooms, halved
16	ounces lobster
2	tablespoons flour
1	teaspoon cornstarch
1	6-ounce can evaporated milk
1	teaspoon white wine
¼	teaspoon white pepper
1	teaspoon salt
¼	teaspoon nutmeg
	Paprika
	Parsley

In large skillet, sauté chicken in butter until tender, about 5 minutes. Add mushrooms and lobster. Sauté 5 minutes. Sprinkle with flour and cornstarch. Add evaporated milk, wine, pepper, salt and nutmeg. Stir until sauce thickens. Transfer to heated platter. Garnish with paprika and parsley.

Crab meat can be substituted for lobster.

SUGGESTED WINE: Round Hill Chardonnay

CHICKEN WITH WILD RICE

PREPARATION TIME: *2 hours, 30 minutes*
YIELD: *10-12 servings*

CHICKEN

5	**whole chicken breasts**
¼	**cup chopped celery**
¼	**cup chopped onion**
⅛	**teaspoon salt**
⅛	**teaspoon pepper**
1	**cup wild rice**
½	**pound mushrooms, sliced**
½	**onion, chopped**
2	**celery stalks, chopped**
2	**tablespoons butter**

In large pot, boil chicken with onion, celery, salt and pepper for about 1½ hours. Cool, remove skin, bone and cut into bite-size pieces. Cook rice according to directions. Sauté mushrooms, celery and onion in butter until tender. Combine vegetables and cooked rice. Spread on bottom of 3-quart casserole. Layer chicken pieces on rice.

SAUCE

2	**cups Creamed Soup Base***
1	**cup mayonnaise**
¼	**cup milk**
1	**tablespoon lemon juice**
1½	**cups shredded sharp Cheddar cheese**
	Paprika

Combine soup base, mayonnaise, milk and lemon juice. Pour over chicken. Sprinkle with cheese, then paprika. Bake at 350 degrees until bubbly, about 45 minutes.

*See recipe for Creamed Soup Base on page 37.

SUGGESTED WINE: Caseres Rioja

CANTONESE CHICKEN WITH GRAPES

PREPARATION TIME: *45 minutes*
YIELD: *4 servings*

2	whole chicken breasts, skinned, boned and cut into 2-inch pieces
1	egg white
1	tablespoon cornstarch
4	cloves garlic, minced
2	tablespoons bean sauce
2	tablespoons water
1	tablespoon sherry
1	cup chicken broth
1	tablespoon soy sauce
1	teaspoon sugar
2	tablespoons cornstarch dissolved in 2 tablespoons water
2	tablespoons peanut oil
2	tablespoons peanut oil
1	cup diced onion
1	small dry red pepper
½	pound seedless red or green grapes

Mix chicken with egg white and cornstarch. In small bowl, combine garlic, bean sauce and water. Set aside. In another small bowl, combine sherry, broth, soy sauce, sugar and dissolved cornstarch. Set aside. Heat 2 tablespoons oil in wok or large skillet. Stir-fry chicken until no longer pink. Transfer to serving platter. Heat remaining 2 tablespoons oil. Stir-fry onion. Add bean sauce mixture. Add chicken. Add sherry mixture. Bring to boil. Crumble red pepper into chicken. Boil 1 minute. Add grapes and boil 1 minute more.

Grapes add an exquisite color. Serve over steamed white rice.

COLD CHICKEN BREASTS WITH YOGURT-WALNUT SAUCE

PREPARATION TIME: *30 minutes plus chilling time*
YIELD: *4 servings*

SAUCE

1	egg yolk
2	tablespoons lemon juice
1	teaspoon salt
½	teaspoon cumin
1	cup firmly packed fresh parsley
1	cup firmly packed fresh spinach leaves
½	cup walnuts
¼	cup olive oil
¾	cup plain yogurt

In blender or food processor, blend together egg yolk, lemon juice, salt, cumin, parsley, spinach and walnuts for 15 seconds. While blending, add stream of olive oil. Stir in yogurt. Chill for 1 hour.

CHICKEN

4	half chicken breasts
2	cups chicken broth
½	lemon, sliced
	Fresh parsley

Skin and bone chicken. Flatten slightly. In large, deep skillet, poach chicken in broth until firm to touch, about 5-10 minutes. Broth should cover chicken. Transfer to shallow glass dish. Pour sauce over chicken. Chill at least 2 hours or overnight. Serve in shallow dish with lemon slices and sprigs of parsley.

Yogurt-Walnut Sauce is also excellent with white fish.

COLD GLAZED CHICKEN

PREPARATION TIME: *1 hour plus marinating and chilling time*
YIELD: *8 servings*

8	half chicken breasts
½	cup lemon juice
2	teaspoons crushed rosemary
⅛	teaspoon salt
4	ounces orange marmalade
2	teaspoons oil
⅛	teaspoon salt (optional)
8	romaine lettuce leaves

Bone chicken, leaving skin intact. In large bowl, mix lemon juice, rosemary and salt. Place breasts in bowl, one at a time, coating each with marinade. Cover bowl and continue marinating in refrigerator about 4 hours. Transfer breasts to roasting pan, skin side up. Bake at 400 degrees until tender, about 40 minutes, basting occasionally with pan drippings. Arrange chicken on serving platter. In small saucepan, heat marmalade, oil and salt until melted. Brush each chicken piece with mixture and refrigerate until cold, about 1 hour. To serve, slip a lettuce leaf under each breast.

An elegant, easy, make-ahead summer entrée.

CORNISH GAME HENS

PREPARATION TIME: *1 hour, 30 minutes*
YIELD: *6 servings*

6	cornish game hens (1-1¼ pounds each)
12	tablespoons butter
¾	cup dry white wine
1	tablespoon tarragon
6	tablespoons tarragon
6	cloves garlic, peeled and halved
3	teaspoons garlic salt

Wash birds inside and out with cold water and drain on paper towel. To make basting sauce, melt butter with wine and 1 tablespoon tarragon. Inside each hen, sprinkle salt, pepper and 1 tablespoon tarragon. Place 2 garlic halves inside each bird. Sprinkle outside of each bird with ½ teaspoon garlic salt and tie legs together. Place birds close together in shallow roasting pan. Roast at 425 degrees until birds are brown and tender, about 1 hour. Baste with sauce every 10 minutes.

Leftover hens are good shredded in a tossed green salad.

SUGGESTED WINE: Tretethen Riesling

GRILLED SAVORY CHICKEN

PREPARATION TIME: *40 minutes plus chilling time*
YIELD: *4 servings*

4	half chicken breasts
¼	teaspoon summer savory (or ¾ teaspoon fresh)
1	teaspoon thyme (or 1 tablespoon fresh)
½	teaspoon sage (or 1½ teaspoons minced fresh)
½	teaspoon rosemary (or 1½ teaspoons minced fresh)
¼	teaspoon marjoram (or ¾ teaspoon fresh)
3	tablespoons minced fresh parsley
1	teaspoon grated lemon rind
⅛	teaspoon allspice
⅛	teaspoon red pepper (cayenne)
⅓	cup olive oil
	Salt and pepper to taste
1	lemon, cut into wedges

Skin, bone and flatten chicken breasts to ¼-inch thickness. Combine all herbs, spices, lemon rind and oil. Rub cutlets with mixture. Arrange in shallow dish. Cover and chill overnight. Sprinkle cutlets with salt and pepper to taste. Grill on well oiled rack over glowing coals for 2-3 minutes on each side. Serve with lemon wedges.

QUICK CHICKEN BOMBAY

PREPARATION TIME: *30 minutes*
YIELD: *5 servings*

1	**tablespoon butter**
1	**cup finely chopped apple (1 medium apple)**
1	**cup sliced celery**
½	**cup chopped onion**
1	**clove garlic, minced**
2	**tablespoons cornstarch**
2-3	**teaspoons curry powder**
1	**teaspoon salt**
½	**cup chicken broth**
2	**cups milk**
2	**cups cooked and diced chicken or turkey**
¼	**pound mushrooms, sliced**

Melt butter in large saucepan. Add apple, celery, onion and garlic. Sauté until mixture is tender. Combine cornstarch, curry, salt and chicken broth. Stir into onion mixture. Add milk. Cook, stirring constantly, until mixture thickens and bubbles. Stir in chicken and mushrooms. Heat thoroughly.

Serve over hot steamed rice. Pass condiments such as raisins, shredded coconut, chopped peanuts, chutney and chopped cucumbers.

SUGGESTED WINE: Lohr Gamay

TROPICAL CHICKEN LIVERS

PREPARATION TIME: *1 hour, 30 minutes*
YIELD: *6-8 servings*

1½	**pounds chicken livers**
¼	**teaspoon garlic powder**
¼	**cup flour**
¼	**teaspoon salt**
¼	**teaspoon pepper**
½	**cup oil**
1	**16-ounce can pineapple chunks**
1	**cup chopped celery**
1	**cup chopped scallion**
½	**cup chopped green bell pepper**
½	**pound mushrooms, sliced**
8	**water chestnuts, thinly sliced**
3	**tablespoons soy sauce**
1	**teaspoon ginger**

Wash and thoroughly dry livers. Sprinkle with garlic powder and set aside for 1 hour. Dust livers with flour, salt and pepper. Sauté in oil for 3 minutes. Drain pineapple and reserve liquid. Add pineapple chunks to livers and brown slightly. Be careful not to overcook. Add all remaining ingredients. Cook about 5 minutes. Vegetables should remain crisp. Stir in 2 tablespoons reserved pineapple juice.

EASY DUCK À L'ORANGE

PREPARATION TIME: *1 hour, 30 minutes*
YIELD: *4 servings*

2	tablespoons flour
1	large oven cooking bag
½	teaspoon salt
1	duck
1	apple, peeled and cored
3	ounces orange juice concentrate
5	ounces current jelly
1	tablespoon minced onion

Place flour inside cooking bag as per bag instructions. Salt duck inside and out. Place apple inside duck. Put duck in bag. Mix orange juice concentrate, jelly, and onion together. Pour over duck. Close bag and bake at 350 degrees for 1 hour, 15 minutes. Remove duck from bag. Use juices as gravy. Discard apple.

Ideal accompaniments are wild rice, fresh green vegetable and a salad.

SUGGESTED WINE: San Martin Chenin Blanc

CHAMPAGNE MUSTARD

PREPARATION TIME: *30 minutes*
YIELD: *12 ounces*

⅔	cup dry Coleman's mustard
1	cup sugar
3	eggs
⅔	cup champagne

In top of double boiler, blend mustard and sugar. In mixing bowl, whisk together eggs and champagne. Mix egg mixture into mustard mixture. Bring water to a boil and beat mixture constantly until thick and foamy, about 7 minutes. Pour immediately into heat resistant jar to stop cooking. Store in refrigerator.

Easy and delicious, but hot!

PINE NUT GRAVY

PREPARATION TIME: *20 minutes*
YIELD: *2 cups*

¼	cup shelled pine nuts
2	tablespoons butter
1	tablespoon minced onion
2	tablespoons flour
1	drop almond extract
⅛	teaspoon grated lemon peel
¾	cup light cream
1	cup chicken broth
½	teaspoon seasoned salt

Lightly sauté pine nuts in 1 tablespoon butter until just golden brown. Set aside. Cook onion in remaining butter until soft. Blend in flour, almond extract and lemon peel. Slowly stir in cream. Add broth. Cook and stir until thick and smooth. Add salt and pine nuts. If thinner gravy is desired, add more broth. Serve hot.

A light, tasty gravy for fried or roasted chicken, pheasant or turkey. Lemon peel can be increased if a stronger flavor is desired.

SESAME-LIME MARINADE

PREPARATION TIME: *15 minutes plus marinating time*
YIELD: *½ cup*

1	tablespoon finely shredded lime peel
⅓	cup lime juice
3	tablespoons oil
1	tablespoon sesame oil
¼	teaspoon salt
2	tablespoons honey
1	teaspoon sesame seeds

Combine lime peel, juice, oils and salt. Pour over chicken or beef and marinate for 1-4 hours. Prepare meat for grill, reserving marinade. Combine ¼ cup marinade, honey and sesame seeds. Baste meat while cooking and again before serving.

This tangy sauce is delicious with chicken or beef kabobs. It keeps the meat moist and flavors the vegetables.

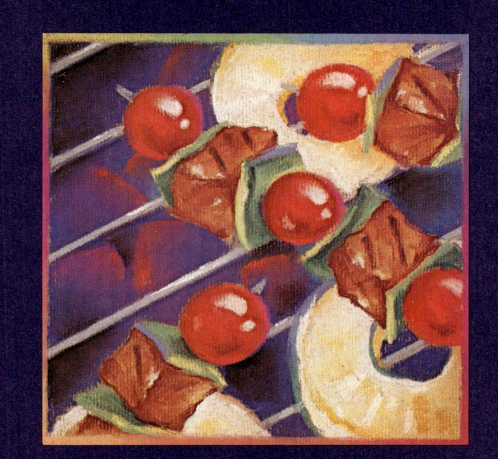

MEATS

Hearty Pleasures

BEEF TENDERLOIN WITH STILTON SAUCE

PREPARATION TIME: *45 minutes*
YIELD: *6 servings*

1	**3-pound beef tenderloin**
	Freshly ground pepper
3	**tablespoons butter**
4	**tablespoons butter, softened**

Pat beef dry and sprinkle generously with pepper, pressing pepper into all sides of meat. In large heavy skillet, melt 3 tablespoons butter and quickly brown meat over high heat. Transfer meat onto rack in roasting pan. Let cool slightly and spread with 4 tablespoons butter. Roast beef at 450 degrees for 25 minutes for rare meat, 30 minutes for medium and 35 minutes for well done. Transfer beef to cutting board. Let cool for 10 minutes.

STILTON SAUCE

¼	**pound Stilton cheese**
6	**tablespoons butter**
1	**cup dry white wine**
1	**cup light cream**
	White pepper to taste

In small bowl, cream together Stilton cheese and 6 tablespoons butter. Add wine to skillet and deglaze over moderately high heat. Reduce wine to ¼ cup. Stir in cheese mixture and cream. Simmer sauce until slightly thickened, about 4 minutes. Season with pepper to taste. Cut beef into ½-inch thick slices and arrange on heated platter. Serve with sauce.

This sauce is good enough for fondue dipping, with crusty French bread!

NO-FAULT PRIME RIB

PREPARATION TIME: *6 hours*
YIELD: *10-12 servings*

	Salt and freshly ground pepper to taste
1	**clove garlic, cut**
1	**10-pound prime rib**

Rub seasoning into roast and place ribs down in roasting pan. Roast at 375 degrees for 1 hour. Turn off oven. Do not open oven door for 4 hours! One hour before serving, set oven to 300 degrees and cook roast for 45 minutes for rare, 50 mintues for medium rare or 55 minutes for medium.

SUGGESTED WINE: Shafer Cabernet Sauvignon

SAUCY BARBECUED BEEF

PREPARATION TIME: *4 hours*
YIELD: *6 servings*

1	1½-2 pound chuck roast
1	8-ounce can tomato sauce
10	ounces beef broth
1	large onion, chopped
1	cup ketchup
¼	cup cider vinegar
¼	cup lemon juice
¼	cup chili sauce
¼	cup orange marmalade
2	tablespoons chopped parsley
	Juice of one orange
1	tablespoon Worcestershire sauce
2	teaspoons paprika
2	teaspoons chili powder
¼	teaspoon oregano
1	clove garlic, minced
	Tabasco sauce to taste

Place roast in Dutch oven. Add water to cover and bring to a boil. Cover, reduce heat and simmer for 1 hour. Lower heat, remove cover and cook an additional hour. Remove and discard all fat and bone from roast. Chop meat and set aside. Combine all remaining ingredients in Dutch oven. Bring to a boil, stirring often. Add meat to sauce. Reduce heat and simmer, uncovered, for 1-1½ hours.

SUGGESTED WINE: Sutter Home White Zinfandel

TOURNEDOS BORDELAISE

PREPARATION TIME: *15 minutes plus marinating time*
YIELD: *6 servings*

6 1¼-inch thick beef tournedos

6 strips bacon

2 cups dry red wine

1 teaspoon thyme

Freshly ground pepper to taste

6 slices day-old bread

6 tablespoons butter

3 tablespoons butter

¼ cup minced shallot

¼ cup minced onion

⅓ cup beef broth

3 tablespoons minced parsley

3 tablespoons butter

Encircle each tournedo with bacon strip and tie with kitchen string. Place beef in glass or ceramic dish in single layer. Add wine and thyme. Marinate in refrigerator for 2 hours, turning occasionally. Remove meat, reserving marinade. Pat meat dry with paper towel. Season generously with pepper, pressing pepper into all sides of meat. Cut 6 bread rounds, same size as tournedos. Melt 6 tablespoons butter in heavy skillet over moderately high heat. Sauté bread, turning until golden. Drain bread rounds and arrange on platter, keeping them warm. Add 3 tablespoons butter to skillet and sear meat over high heat about 3 minutes on each side for rare meat, 4 minutes for medium and 5 minutes for well-done. Remove and discard kitchen string and bacon. Arrange each tournedo on a bread round. In same skillet, sauté shallot and onion until soft. Add reserved marinade and reduce to 1 cup. Stir in broth and parsley. Simmer mixture for 3 minutes. Remove skillet from heat, swirl in 3 tablespoons butter and pour sauce over meat.

HOT STUFFED BUNS

PREPARATION TIME: *3 hours, 30 minutes*
YIELD: *8-10 buns*

1	**package dry yeast**
¼	**cup sugar**
1	**cup luke warm water**
1½	**cups flour**
2	**eggs, beaten**
¼	**cup shortening**
1	**teaspooon salt**
1½-2½	**cups flour**
3	**tablespoons shortening**
1	**medium onion, chopped**
½	**head cabbage, chopped**
1	**tablespoon salt**
½	**teaspoon pepper**
1	**pound ground beef**

Mix yeast, sugar, water and 1½ cups flour. Let sit 45 minutes or until frothy. Add eggs, ½ cup shortening, 1 teaspoon salt and 1½-2½ cups flour to make a soft dough. Knead 5 minutes and let rise 1½ hours or until doubled. Melt remaining shortening in skillet. Add onion, cabbage, salt and pepper. Cook until tender. In separate skillet, brown ground beef and add to cabbage mixture. Cool. Roll dough to ¼-inch thickness. Cut into 4-inch squares. Place 2-3 tablespoons filling on each square. Bring corners of square together and pinch openings shut. Place seam side down on greased cookie sheet. Let rise 1 hour. Bake at 350 degrees for 35 minutes. Serve hot.

Wrap in foil, then in newspaper, and take to a picnic or ball game. Serve with pickles, carrots and celery sticks and finish with frosted brownies.
Also good cold in packed lunches.
May be frozen.

HEARTY CHILI

PREPARATION TIME: *3 hours, 30 minutes*
YIELD: *8 servings*

2	**pounds ground beef**
4	**cups water**
2	**medium onions**
2	**8-ounce cans tomato sauce**
5	**whole allspice**
½	**teaspoon red pepper (cayenne)**
1	**teaspoon cumin**
4	**tablespoons chili powder**
½	**ounce bitter chocolate**
4	**cloves garlic, crushed**
2	**tablespoons red wine vinegar**
1	**large bay leaf**
2	**teaspoons Worcestershire sauce**
1½	**teaspoons salt**
5	**whole cloves**
1	**teaspoon cinnamon**

In large saucepan, cover meat with water. Stir until beef separates. Boil slowly for 30 minutes. Stir in all other ingredients. Bring to a boil, reduce heat and simmer, covered, for 2½-3 hours. During the last hour, chili may be uncovered until desired consistency is reached. Remove bay leaf before serving.

Refrigerate chili overnight so that fat may be removed before serving.
Great topped with grated Cheddar cheese and chopped onions.

GOLDEN CROWN MEAT LOAF

PREPARATION TIME: *1 hour, 30 minutes*
YIELD: *6 servings*

MEAT LOAF
1 cup fine bread crumbs

1½ pounds lean ground beef

4 egg yolks

1½ teaspoons salt

2 tablespoons Dijon mustard

1 tablespoon horseradish

¼ cup minced scallions

¼ cup minced green bell pepper

⅓ cup tomato sauce

¼ teaspoon freshly ground pepper

TOPPING
3 egg whites

¼ teaspoon cream of tartar

1½ tablespoons Dijon mustard

Combine all meat loaf ingredients and blend together well. Pack into greased 2-quart soufflé dish and bake at 350 degrees for 30 minutes. Remove excess fat and liquid with bulb baster.

In medium bowl, beat egg whites until foamy, add cream of tartar and continue beating until stiff. Gently fold in mustard and swirl mixture over meat loaf. Bake 25-30 minutes longer, until topping is puffed and golden.

MEATBALLS WITH TOMATO CREAM SAUCE

PREPARATION TIME: *2 hours, 15 minutes*
YIELD: *6 servings*

MEATBALLS

4	slices bacon, minced
⅔	cup minced onion
2	cloves garlic, minced
½	pound ground chuck
½	pound ground pork
¼	cup heavy cream
¼	cup fresh bread crumbs
1	egg, lightly beaten
1	tablespoon fresh dill
2	teaspoons grated lemon rind
	Salt and ground pepper to taste

TOMATO CREAM SAUCE

⅔	cup beef broth
⅔	cup sour cream
⅔	cup tomato sauce
2	tablespoons lemon juice
	Salt and ground pepper to taste
2	tablespoons butter
2	tablespoons oil
1	tablespoon flour
1	tablespoon fresh dill

In large, heavy skillet, fry bacon with onion and garlic until onion is soft, about 10 minutes. In large bowl, combine beef and pork with bacon mixture and remaining meatball ingredients. Form into 1-inch balls, cover and refrigerate for 1 hour.

In small bowl, combine beef broth, sour cream, tomato sauce, lemon juice and salt and pepper. Set aside. In large skillet, sauté meat balls in 2 tablespoons butter and oil, over moderately high heat, until browned, about 5 minutes. Transfer with a slotted spoon to a dish and keep warm. Reserve 2 tablespoons fat, taking care not to discard brown bits.

To same skillet, add flour. Cook and stir roux over low heat for 4 minutes. Stir in sauce. Add meatballs. Cook mixture, covered, over very low heat for 10 minutes, being careful not to boil. Transfer meatballs and sauce to a heated serving dish and sprinkle with dill.

ROAST VEAL WITH ROQUEFORT STUFFING

PREPARATION TIME: *2 hours plus fermenting time*
YIELD: *4-6 servings*

1½	**cups heavy cream**
5	**tablespoons sour cream**
6	**strips bacon**
1	**3-pound boneless veal roast**
3	**cups finely chopped walnuts (about ¾ pound)**
1	**cup unsalted butter**
¾	**pound Roquefort cheese**
⅓	**cup cognac**
	Salt and white pepper to taste

In small bowl, combine cream and sour cream. Beat for 1 minute. Cover mixture securely and let sit at room temperature until thickened, at least 6 hours. Refrigerate until ready to use. Wrap bacon around veal roast and tie securely with kitchen string. Roast veal on rack in shallow roasting pan at 400 degrees for 45 minutes. Remove from oven and lower temperature to 325 degrees. Blend walnuts, butter and Roquefort cheese into a paste. Remove kitchen string from roast and thickly slice veal, downward, but not all the way through. Spread cheese mixture between slices and retie roast lengthwise. Return to oven and cook for 30-35 minutes longer. Remove veal to a hot serving platter and discard string and bacon. Deglaze pan with cognac and add cream mixture. Stir over medium heat until well blended. Salt and pepper to taste.

STUFFED GERMAN VEAL ROAST

PREPARATION TIME: *4 hours*
YIELD: *6-8 servings*

1	**3-4-pound boneless veal loin roast**
6	**slices bacon, diced**
2	**onions, chopped**
1	**cup rice**
2	**cups chicken broth**
2	**eggs**
½	**teaspoon nutmeg**
1	**teaspoon rosemary**
2	**tablespoons chopped fresh parsley**
	Salt and pepper to taste
½	**cup flour seasoned with salt, pepper, paprika and garlic powder**
2	**tablespoons flour**
1	**cup milk**
½	**cup sour cream**
2	**tablespoons dry white wine**

Have a butcher cut a pocket into the veal roast. In heavy skillet, sauté diced bacon. Remove bacon with a slotted spoon and set aside. Add onions to skillet and sauté until golden. Add rice and chicken broth. Stir and let mixture steam for 30 minutes. Let rice cool, then toss with eggs, nutmeg, rosemary, parsley and bacon. Salt and pepper to taste. Stuff pocket with this mixture and sew pocket up with needle and thread. If meat is not fat, rub with butter. Dredge roast in seasoned flour. Roast in oven, uncovered, at 300 degrees for 25-30 minutes per pound. When meat is done, remove from pan to heated platter. Make pan gravy with the drippings by adding 2 tablespoons flour and 1 cup milk, stirring until smooth. Remove gravy from heat and add sour cream and wine. Reheat gravy, but do not let it boil. Slice roast and serve with gravy.

Serve with stuffed tomatoes, brioche and hot apple strudel for a real German feast!

SUGGESTED WINE: Schloss Vollrads Kabinett

VEAL À LA FORESTIÈRE

PREPARATION TIME: *40 minutes*
YIELD: *4 servings*

1½	pounds veal cutlets
1	clove garlic, flattened
	Flour
4	tablespoons butter
½	pound fresh mushrooms, thinly sliced
½	teaspoon salt
	Pepper to taste
⅓	cup dry vermouth
	Lemon juice
	Snipped parsley

Pound cutlets to ¼-inch thickness and cut into 2-inch pieces. Rub each piece with garlic and sprinkle with flour. In large skillet, melt butter and sauté veal on both sides until golden. Add mushrooms, salt, pepper and vermouth. Cover and cook over low heat for 20 minutes. Sprinkle with lemon juice and parsley.

BREADED VEAL MARSALA

PREPARATION TIME: *30 minutes*
YIELD: *6 servings*

12	veal scallops
3	eggs, beaten
½	cup flour
1	cup seasoned breadcrumbs
6	tablespoons butter
3	tablespoons olive oil
½	cup beef broth
½	cup Marsala wine

Pound scallops between wax paper. Dip each scallop in egg, then flour, then egg again, then breadcrumbs. Melt butter in heavy skillet and add oil. When hot and bubbling, brown scallops quickly on both sides. Place on platter and keep warm. Add broth and wine to skillet. Return meat to skillet and simmer for 3 minutes.

SUGGESTED WINE: Brunello di Montalcino

VEAL SCALLOPS AND GRAPES

PREPARATION TIME: *30 minutes*
YIELD: *4 servings*

8	**veal scallops**
	Salt and freshly ground pepper
⅓	**cup flour**
3	**tablespoons olive oil**
2	**tablespoons butter**
1	**cup Sauterne**
¾	**cup chicken broth**
1	**cup seedless green grapes, peeled**
2	**tablespoons butter, softened**

Pound veal scallops between wax paper. Sprinkle with salt and pepper and dust lightly with flour. In heavy skillet, melt butter and add oil. Add veal and cook 2 minutes on each side. Transfer scallops to heated platter and keep warm. Add Sauterne and broth to skillet. Heat to reduce liquid by half. Lower heat and add peeled grapes. Simmer 3 minutes. Remove sauce from heat. Swirl in 2 tablespoons butter. Serve sauce over veal.

VEAL WITH LEMON CREAM SAUCE

PREPARATION TIME: *1 hour*
YIELD: *4 servings*

2	**1-pound veal fillets**
2	**tablespoons butter**
⅓	**cup minced shallots**
4	**tablespoons butter**
2	**teaspoons tarragon**
⅔	**cup dry vermouth**
2	**tablespoons lemon juice**
1	**cup heavy cream**
	Salt and white pepper to taste
⅓	**cup heavy cream**

In large, heavy skillet, brown veal on both sides in 2 tablespoons butter. Transfer veal to rack in shallow roasting pan. Roast at 450 degrees for 30 minutes. In same skillet, sauté shallot in 4 tablespoons butter over moderate heat until softened. Stir in tarragon and cook for 30 seconds. Stir in vermouth and lemon juice and combine well. Add heavy cream and reduce sauce over moderately high heat to about 1 cup. Add salt and pepper to taste and keep warm. Transfer veal to cutting board and cut crosswise into thin slices. Swirl heavy cream into sauce and serve over veal.

BROILED LAMB WITH KIWI

PREPARATION TIME: *25 minutes plus marinating time*
YIELD: *6 servings*

2 **tablespoons oil**	In ceramic or glass bowl, combine 2 tablespoons oil, lemon juice and soy sauce. Marinate lamb, tossing twice, for 2 hours. Remove lamb, reserving marinade. In small bowl, combine 3 tablespoons oil, brown sugar and reserved marinade. Toss lamb and kiwi in mixture. Place lamb and kiwi in shallow baking dish. Dribble with any reserved mixture. Broil until done, about 8 minutes.
2 **tablespoons lemon juice**	
2 **tablespoons soy sauce**	
2 **pounds boneless leg of lamb, cut into 1-inch cubes**	
3 **tablespoons oil**	
4 **tablespoons brown sugar**	
8 **kiwi, peeled and cut into ¼-inch slices**	

CURRIED LAMB KABOBS

PREPARATION TIME: *1 hour, 15 minutes*
YIELD: *4 servings*

½ **teaspoon saffron threads**	Sprinkle saffron threads in small ungreased skillet. Toast for 30 seconds, shaking constantly, over low medium heat. Remove threads to small bowl. When cool enough to touch, crumble them with your fingers. Pour in 1 teaspoon boiling water and soak for 3 minutes. In large bowl, combine lamb, onions, flour, almonds, lemon juice, yogurt, curry powder and salt. Add saffron and water and mix well. Let mixture stand uncovered, at room temperature, for 15-20 minutes. Roll lamb mixture into 14-16 equal balls and thread them on skewers. Broil or grill kabobs for 5 minutes on each side. Serve kabobs on a platter of sliced onions and tomatoes and sprinkle with ½ teaspoon curry powder.
1 **tablespoon boiling water**	
1 **pound ground lamb**	
1 **cup finely chopped onions**	
¼ **cup flour**	
½ **cup finely chopped almonds**	
3 **tablespoons lemon juice**	
2 **tablespoons plain yogurt**	
2 **teaspoons curry powder**	
2 **teaspoons salt**	
1 **onion, thinly sliced**	
2 **tomatoes, thinly sliced**	
½ **teaspoon curry powder**	

SUGGESTED WINE: Demestica Red

LAMB CHOPS IN SORREL CREAM

PREPARATION TIME: *30 minutes*
YIELD: *4 servings*

8	**1-inch-thick rib lamb chops**
2	**tablespoons butter**
1½	**cups shredded sorrel leaves**
½	**cup dry white wine**
½	**cup heavy cream**
1	**tablespoon minced fresh mint (or 1 teaspoon dried)**
	Salt and white pepper to taste

Trim fat from lamb chops. In large skillet, sauté chops in butter, over high heat, for 3 minutes on each side. Transfer to heated platter and keep warm. Pour fat from skillet and add sorrel leaves and white wine. Stir liquid over high heat until reduced to about ¼ cup. Add heavy cream and mint, stirring until thickened, about 5 minutes. Add salt and pepper to taste. Pour sauce over chops.

ROLLED GRAPE LEAVES

PREPARATION TIME: *3 hours*
YIELD: *15-20 servings*

2	**cups rice**
24	**ounces tomato juice**
½	**pound pine nuts, shelled**
3	**large onions, chopped**
4	**tablespoons butter**
3	**pounds ground lamb**
	Pepper to taste
2	**teaspoons allspice**
1	**teaspoon cinnamon**
2	**cloves garlic, crushed**
1	**teaspoon seasoned salt**
1	**teaspoon nutmeg**
3	**jars grape leaves**
2½	**48-ounce cans tomato juice**
4	**lemons**

Cook rice according to package directions and add 24 ounces tomato juice and pine nuts. Set aside. In large skillet, sauté onions in butter until golden. Pour off fat. Add lamb and cook until no longer pink. Pepper to taste. In large bowl, combine rice, lamb and spices. Mix well. Unroll grape leaves and, with tongs, dip leaves into hot water. Roll a ball of rice-meat mixture and place at bottom of grape leaf. Fold grape leaf up from bottom. Fold edges toward middle and continue rolling. Place stuffed grape leaves in three 9 x 18-inch baking dishes and completely cover with remaining tomato juice. Squeeze lemons over top. Bake at 350 degrees for 30 minutes. Cool and cover to prevent blackening of grape leaves.

LAMB NOISETTES WITH ARTICHOKE BOTTOMS

PREPARATION TIME: *30 minutes*
YIELD: *6 servings*

LAMB

4	**tablespoons butter**
6	**¾-inch-thick lamb noisettes**
	Salt and freshly ground pepper to taste
3	**tablespoons butter**
6	**artichoke bottoms**

BÉARNAISE SAUCE

½	**cup sherry vinegar (or white wine vinegar)**
¼	**cup dry white vermouth**
1	**tablespoon finely chopped shallot**
½	**teaspoon dried tarragon**
⅛	**teaspoon salt**
3	**egg yolks**
1	**cup butter, melted**

In large skillet, melt 4 tablespoons butter over moderately high heat. Sear lamb quickly for 3 minutes on each side. Sprinkle with salt and pepper and arrange on heated platter. In same skillet, melt 3 tablespoons butter and sauté artichoke bottoms for 3 minutes. Place one artichoke bottom on each noisette.

In small saucepan, combine vinegar, vermouth, shallot, tarragon and salt. Bring to a boil, lower heat and simmer, reducing sauce to ¼ cup. Cool to room temperature. Strain mixture into double boiler. Whisk in egg yolks and beat until thick and creamy. Remove pan from heat. Whisking constantly, add melted butter, 1 tablespoon at a time. Fill each artichoke bottom with Sauce Béarnaise.

SUGGESTED WINE: Chateau Pavie Red Bordeaux

PHYLLO LAMB WITH MINT SAUCE

PREPARATION TIME: *1 hour, 30 minutes*
YIELD: *8 servings*

LAMB

2 **onions, minced**

2 **tablespoons olive oil**

2½ **pounds ground lamb**

¼ **cup minced fresh mint, (or 4 teaspoons dried)**

1 **teaspoon cinnamon**

⅛ **teaspoon nutmeg**

Salt to taste

¾ **cup pine nuts, shelled**

2 **tablespoons butter**

1½ **cups butter, melted**

20 **phyllo pastry sheets**

In large skillet, sauté onions in olive oil until soft. Add lamb and cook until no longer pink. Drain fat and stir in mint, cinnamon, nutmeg and salt. In small skillet, brown pine nuts in 2 tablespoons butter. Add nuts to lamb mixture. Let cool to room temperature. Stack phyllo sheets between 2 dampened tea towels. Brush a 13 x 9 x 2-inch baking pan with butter. Brush 4 sheets of phyllo each with butter. Line pan with these sheets, allowing the ends to extend beyond the edge of the pan. Spread ¼ of the lamb mixture on the phyllo. Continue to layer lamb mixture and 4 sheets of phyllo in the same manner, ending with a layer of lamb mixture. Fold the overhanging ends over the lamb mixture and top with remaining sheets of buttered phyllo. Tuck the ends down inside the edge of the pan. Bake at 375 degrees until phyllo is golden, about 45 minutes. Serve with mint sauce on the side.

MINT SAUCE

1 **cup white vinegar**

½ **cup sugar**

1 **cup minced fresh mint leaves**

In a small saucepan, heat vinegar and sugar until mixture boils and sugar dissolves. Pour hot sauce over the mint and let stand at least 1 hour.

CURRIED PORK SANDWICHES

PREPARATION TIME: *1 hour*
YIELD: *10 servings*

1	large onion, chopped
2	cloves garlic, minced
4	tablespoons oil
2	pounds lean ground pork
¾	teaspoon ginger
1	teaspoon curry powder
2	tablespoons soy sauce
⅓	cup sweet pickle relish
4	drops Tabasco sauce
1½	teaspoons sugar
1	teaspoon white vinegar
	Salt to taste
¾	cup plain yogurt
10	pita breads
2	tomatoes, chopped (optional)
1	cup plain yogurt (optional)

Sauté onion and garlic in oil until onions are transparent. Add pork and cook over low heat, stirring occasionally, until meat is lightly browned, about 20 minutes. Drain off fat. Add ginger, curry powder, soy sauce, pickle relish, Tabasco sauce, sugar, vinegar and salt. Blend and continue cooking over low heat for 10-15 minutes. Add ¾ cup yogurt. Stir and heat just under boiling. To serve, cut pita breads into halves. Fill pockets with meat mixture. If desired, add chopped tomato and additional yogurt.

PORK ROAST WITH CARMELIZED APPLES

PREPARATION TIME: *3 hours*
YIELD: *8 servings*

PORK ROAST
1 tablespoon salt

1 clove garlic, crushed (optional)

½ teaspoon Hungarian paprika

Pepper to taste

1 4-pound rolled loin of pork, rinsed and patted dry

Combine salt, garlic, paprika and pepper in small bowl. Rub seasoning mixture over roast. Position oven rack in center of oven. Place meat on small rack in a shallow pan. Roast at 425 degrees for 1 hour.

GLAZE
½ small onion, minced

1 cup apple jelly

1 teaspoon dry mustard

Combine onion, apple jelly and mustard. Mix well. Brush pork generously with glaze. Reduce oven to 375 degrees and continue roasting until thermometer inserted in center of meat registers 170 degrees, about 1-1½ hours. Remove roast from oven. Cover with foil and let stand 30 minutes before serving.

APPLES
5 tart apples, peeled, halved, cored and sliced

⅔ cup sugar

¼ cup unsalted butter

In large bowl lightly toss apples in sugar. Melt butter in large skillet over medium high heat. Add apples. Reduce heat to medium and cook, lifting and turning apples occasionally, until carmelized, about 25 minutes.
Slice pork and serve on heated platter, surrounded by apples.

PORK ST. TAMMANY

PREPARATION TIME: *2 hours, 30 minutes*
YIELD: *8-10 servings*

1	**6-ounce package rice**
½	**cup boiling water**
½	**cup dried apricots**
½	**clove garlic, crushed**
2	**scallions, finely chopped**
½	**cup chopped fresh mushrooms**
¼	**cup chopped green bell pepper**
2	**tablespoons butter**
3	**tablespoons chopped pecans**
1	**tablespoon chopped fresh parsley**
⅛	**teaspoon salt**
⅛	**teaspoon pepper**
	Red pepper (cayenne) to taste
4	**1½-pound boneless pork tenderloins**
4	**slices bacon**

Cook rice according to package directions. Set aside. Pour boiling water over apricots and let stand 20 minutes, then drain. In large skillet, sauté garlic, scallions, mushrooms and green bell pepper in butter until tender. Add rice, apricots, pecans, parsley and seasonings. Stir until combined. Cut a lengthwise slit on top of each tenderloin. Spoon ½ of stuffing into openings in 2 tenderloins. Place other 2 tenderloins with cut side over stuffing. Tie securely together with kitchen string and top with two slices of bacon. Place an aluminum foil tent over the meat and roast at 325 degrees for 1½-2 hours. Remove foil the last 30-40 minutes. Remove from oven and let stand 5 minutes.

SUGGESTED WINE: Raymond Chenin Blanc

STIR-FRIED PORK AND PEANUTS

PREPARATION TIME: *15 minutes plus chilling time*
YIELD: *4 servings*

1	**pound boneless pork loin, thinly sliced**
1	**tablespoon cornstarch**
2	**tablespoons dry sherry**
2	**tablespoons soy sauce**
¼	**cup peanut oil**
2	**tablespoons sliced scallions**
1	**clove garlic, crushed**
3	**carrots, thinly sliced and blanched**
1	**green bell pepper, cut into 2-inch strips**
½	**cup chicken broth**
1	**tablespoon dark brown sugar, firmly packed**
½	**cup unsalted peanuts**

Toss pork with mixture of cornstarch, sherry and soy sauce. Refrigerate at least 1 hour. Heat peanut oil in large skillet or wok over high heat. Add scallions and garlic, and stir-fry 1 minute. Add pork mixture and stir-fry until meat loses its pink color. Mix in carrots and green bell pepper. Cook and stir 2 minutes. Combine broth and brown sugar. Add to skillet mixture, stirring until sauce thickens. Stir in peanuts.

Chicken breasts may be substituted for pork.

SUGGESTED WINE: Haywood White Riesling

HAM LOAF EN CROÛTE

PREPARATION TIME: *1 hour plus chilling time*
YIELD: *8 servings*

HAM LOAF

1	large onion, finely chopped
3	tablespoons butter
⅓	pound mushrooms, finely chopped
2½	pounds lean ground ham
1	teaspoon grated lemon peel
2	eggs, lightly beaten
1½	cups shredded Swiss cheese
⅛	teaspoon nutmeg
	Salt and freshly ground pepper to taste

In large skillet, sauté onion in 3 tablespoons butter until golden. Add mushrooms and sauté for 1 minute. Let cool. In large glass or ceramic bowl, combine sautéed ingredients with ham, lemon peel, eggs, cheese, nutmeg, salt and pepper. Chill.

SOUR CREAM PASTRY

2	cups flour
⅔	cup butter
1	egg white
⅓	cup sour cream
1	egg white, lightly beaten

Place flour in bowl or food processor and cut in butter until fine and crumbly. Beat egg white with sour cream and stir into flour mixture. Form mixture into a ball. Wrap in wax paper and chill 1 hour. Roll chilled pastry into a 14 x 16-inch rectangle. Form meat into a 10 x 4 x 3-inch loaf. Place meat loaf on the pastry rectangle and fold sides up over the loaf so they meet in a seam across the top. Fold the ends up. Turn the loaf, seam side down, onto greased baking sheet. Brush lightly with beaten egg white. Bake at 375 degrees until pastry is golden, about 35 minutes.

SHALLOT SAUCE

3	tablespoons chopped shallots
1	cup sour cream
	Salt and white pepper to taste

In small bowl, combine Shallot Sauce ingredients. Serve loaf sliced, hot or cold, with Shallot Sauce.

SUGGESTED WINE: Dry Creek Chenin Blanc

APPLE SAUSAGE RING

PREPARATION TIME: *1 hour, 15 minutes*
YIELD: *8 servings*

2 pounds ground pork sausage	Combine all ingredients and mix thoroughly. Press lightly into greased 6-cup ring mold and turn out onto shallow baking pan. Bake at 350 degrees for 1 hour.
2 eggs, lightly beaten	
½ cup milk	
1½ cups herb stuffing	
¼ cup minced onion	
1 cup finely chopped apple (about 1 large apple)	

ITALIAN SAUSAGE QUICHE

PREPARATION TIME: *1 hour*
YIELD: *4-6 servings*

1 9-inch unbaked pastry shell	Prick pastry shell with a fork. Partially bake at 400 degrees until just beginning to brown, about 5-8 minutes. Brown sausage in small skillet. Transfer to medium bowl. Add onion to pan drippings and sauté over low heat until tender. Add onion to sausage. Stir in eggs, evaporated milk, whole milk, parsley, salt, nutmeg and peppers. Sprinkle cheese on bottom of pastry shell and pour in sausage mixture. Bake at 425 degrees for 10 minutes. Reduce heat to 350 degrees and continue baking 25 minutes longer. Let stand 10 minutes before serving.
½ cup coarsely chopped sweet Italian sausage (approximately 2 small sausages)	
½ cup chopped onion	
4 eggs, lightly beaten	
1 cup evaporated milk	
¾ cup milk	
1 tablespoon chopped parsley	
½ teaspoon salt	
⅛ teaspoon nutmeg	
⅛ teaspoon red pepper (cayenne)	
⅛ teaspoon pepper	
½ pound Muenster cheese, shredded	

BARBECUE SAUCE

PREPARATION TIME: *40 minutes*
YIELD: *2½ cups*

1	**medium onion, finely chopped**
2	**tablespoons butter**
4	**tablespoons lemon juice**
1	**tablespoon brown sugar**
1	**cup ketchup**
1	**tablespoon Worcestershire sauce**
1	**teaspoon dry mustard**
½	**cup finely chopped celery**
½	**cup hot water**
1	**teaspoon salt**
¼	**teaspoon red pepper (cayenne)**
¼	**teaspoon black pepper**

In medium heavy saucepan sauté onion in butter. Add remaining ingredients, except salt and peppers. Simmer 30 minutes. Add salt and peppers. Simmer 5 minutes.

Terrific on chicken or hamburgers.

CURRY MINT SAUCE

PREPARATION TIME: *10 minutes*
YIELD: *2 cups*

1½ cups sour cream	Combine all ingredients. Chill.
Zest of 1 lemon	
1 teaspoon curry powder	
¼ teaspoon tumeric	
1 tablespoon honey	
6 tablespoons heavy cream	
1 tablespoon chopped fresh mint	
Salt to taste	
White pepper to taste	

From Chef Neil McLaren, at Westin La Paloma. This sauce adds great taste to a variety of foods, such as vegetable turnovers, fresh vegetables, lamb and meat pastries. Limited only by your imagination!

HORSERADISH CREAM

PREPARATION TIME: *5 minutes plus chilling time*
YIELD: *2 cups*

1 4-ounce bottle prepared horseradish, drained and squeezed dry in kitchen towel	In a small bowl, combine horseradish, vinegar, sugar and salt. Mix together well. Fold in whipped cream. Chill until serving time.
1 tablespoon wine vinegar	
1 teaspoon sugar	
½ teaspoon salt	
1 cup heavy cream, whipped	

A mellow but very tasty sauce for any roast beef.

MANGO SAUCE

PREPARATION TIME: *30 minutes*
YIELD: *1 cup*

4	**fresh serrano or jalapeño chilies, finely chopped (about 2 tablespoons)**
6	**tablespoons lime juice**
¼	**cup white wine vinegar**
3	**tablespoons finely chopped shallots**
½	**cup water**
1	**mango, peeled and pitted**
¾	**cup butter, cut into 1-tablespoon pieces**
¼	**teaspoon salt**

In non-corrodible skillet, place chilies, lime juice, vinegar, shallot and water. Bring to a boil over high heat and boil until liquid is reduced to 2½ tablespoons, about 5 minutes. Remove from heat and set aside. Purée mango in blender or food processor and set aside. Bring chili-vinegar mixture back to a boil. Reduce heat and cook 30 seconds. Whisk in butter, 1 tablespoon at a time. Strain sauce into saucepan. Whisk in mango purée and salt. Reheat briefly over low heat. Do not allow to boil.

Serve sauce with grilled pork or veal chops which have been basted in lime juice and butter.

PEAR MUSTARD SAUCE

PREPARATION TIME: *20 minutes*
YIELD: *2 cups*

4	**pears, peeled and diced**
1	**cup water**
1	**tablespoon honey**
⅓	**cup vinegar**
⅓	**cup Dijon mustard**

Cook pears in water until soft, stirring frequently to keep from burning. Drain and cool slightly. Add honey, vinegar and mustard. Purée in blender or food processor until smooth. Store in covered glass dish in refrigerator.

Garnish with fresh mint and serve hot or cold to accompany roast pork, lamb or veal.

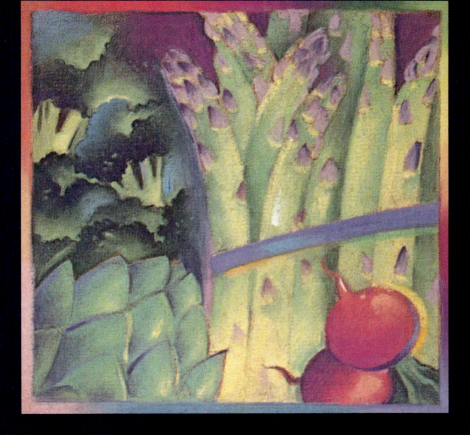

VEGETABLES, RICE & PASTA

Harvested Pleasures

ARTICHOKE QUICHE

PREPARATION TIME: *1 hour, 15 minutes*
YIELD: *4-6 servings*

1	**9-inch pie shell**
2	**6-ounce jars marinated artichokes**
½	**cup chopped onion**
1	**clove garlic, minced**
4	**eggs**
¼	**cup bread crumbs**
¼	**teaspoon salt**
⅛	**teaspoon pepper**
⅛	**teaspoon oregano**
2	**cups shredded Cheddar cheese**
2	**tablespoons chopped parsley**

Prick pie shell with fork. Bake at 400 degrees until just beginning to brown, about 5 minutes. Drain artichokes, reserving marinade in small saucepan. Cook onion and garlic in marinade for 5 minutes. In large bowl, beat eggs. Add bread crumbs, salt, pepper and oregano. Stir in cheese, parsley, artichokes and onion-garlic marinade. Pour filling into pie shell and bake at 325 degrees for 45 minutes. Let set 10 minutes before serving.

ITALIAN ASPARAGUS

PREPARATION TIME: *1 hour*
YIELD: *4 servings*

1	**pound fresh asparagus**
1	**onion, thinly sliced**
2	**tablespoons chopped celery**
1	**large tomato, sliced**
⅛	**teaspoon salt**
¼	**teaspoon pepper**
¼	**teaspoon oregano**
⅛	**teaspoon thyme**
¼	**cup bread crumbs**
2	**tablespoons grated Parmesan cheese**
3	**tablespoons butter, melted**

Line 9 x 13-inch pan with asparagus. Top with onion, celery and tomato. Sprinkle with seasonings, bread crumbs and cheese. Drizzle with butter. Cover and bake at 375 degrees for 45 minutes.

STUFFED ARTICHOKES

PREPARATION TIME: *1 hour, 30 minutes*
YIELD: *4 servings*

4	artichokes
2	cups bread crumbs
¼	cup grated Romano cheese
1	teaspoon salt
¼	teaspoon pepper
1	small clove garlic, minced
4	tablespoons parsley flakes
2	eggs
¼	cup water
¼	cup oil

Cut tops of artichokes flat. Trim tips of remaining leaves. Cut off stems so artichokes stand upright. Place in covered casserole with sides touching. In small bowl, mix all dry ingredients. Pour an equal amount of mixture over each artichoke, coaxing it between leaves. Beat eggs with ¼ cup water. Pour over artichokes. This will mix with bread crumb mixture while cooking and form "stuffing." Drizzle artichokes with oil. Pour a 3-inch bath of salt water around artichokes. Stove-top method: Cover. Bring water to boil. Simmer for 1 hour or until leaves are tender and pull away easily.
Oven method: Cover. Bake at 350 degrees for 1 hour or until leaves are tender and pull away easily.
Microwave oven method: Cover. Cook on high power for 20 minutes. Serve hot or cold.

MARINATED ASPARAGUS

PREPARATION TIME: *15 minutes plus chilling time*
YIELD: *4 servings*

12	fresh asparagus spears
2	tablespoons olive oil
2	tablespoons cider vinegar
¼	teaspoon salt
1	teaspoon honey
1	bay leaf

Steam asparagus until tender but still crisp. Drain. Beat together oil, vinegar, salt and honey. Pour over asparagus in shallow dish. Add bay leaf. Cover and refrigerate several hours or overnight. Remove bay leaf before serving.

FOUR BEAN CASSEROLE

PREPARATION TIME: *2 hours, 15 minutes*
YIELD: *10-12 servings*

1 **16-ounce can pinto beans**

1 **16-ounce can kidney beans**

1 **16-ounce can pork and beans**

1 **10-ounce package frozen Italian beans or lima beans, thawed**

4 **slices bacon, chopped**

6 **scallions, chopped**

1 **green bell pepper, chopped**

1 **8-ounce jar chili sauce**

¾ **cup brown sugar**

Drain all beans well. Mix together. Fry bacon pieces with scallions and pepper. In oven-proof serving dish, mix beans with bacon mixture, chili sauce and brown sugar. Bake uncovered at 325 degrees, for 2 hours.

GREEN BEAN BUNDLES

PREPARATION TIME: *20 minutes*
YIELD: *6 servings*

¾ **pound green beans**

1 **tablespoon lemon juice**

¼ **teaspoon salt**

Pepper to taste

3 **tablespoons olive oil**

Pimento strips

Trim green beans and cut into julienne strips. Steam until just tender, about 4 minutes. Transfer beans to a bowl and let cool. In another bowl, combine lemon juice, salt, pepper and olive oil, beating well. Pour dressing over beans to coat. Divide into bundles and wrap with strips of pimento.

SUMMER LIMA BEANS

PREPARATION TIME: *15 minutes plus chilling time*
YIELD: *4 servings*

1	**10-ounce package frozen baby lima beans**
3	**tablespoons chopped chives**
1	**small clove garlic, minced**
⅛	**teaspoon salt**
¼	**teaspoon pepper**
½	**cup sour cream**
2	**tablespoons chopped pimentos**

Cook beans according to package directions. Drain. Toss beans with chives, garlic, salt, pepper and sour cream. Top with pimentos. Chill and serve.

GLAZED MATCHSTICK BEETS

PREPARATION TIME: *1 hour*
YIELD: *8 servings*

2½	**cups pear nectar**
2½	**cups water**
3	**tablespoons butter**
1½	**pounds young beets, peeled and julienne cut to matchstick size**
½	**teaspoon dry mustard**
½	**teaspoon salt**
½	**teaspoon ginger**
1	**cup water**

Bring pear nectar and 2½ cups water to boil. Melt butter in large deep skillet over medium high heat. Add beets and spices and blend well. Pour boiling pear nectar over beets and return to boil. Cook, stirring often, until beets are tender, about 40 minutes. Add remaining water if necessary.

If sweeter beets are preferred, add up to 2 tablespoons sugar.

BROCCOLI MOUSSE WITH LEMON BUTTER SAUCE

PREPARATION TIME: *2 hours*
YIELD: *4-6 servings*

MOUSSE
2	**pounds broccoli**
¼	**cup heavy cream**
1	**egg**
	Salt and freshly ground pepper to taste
	Butter

Separate broccoli flowerettes from stems. Trim and peel stems, then slice thinly. Blanch flowerettes and stems separately in large pot of boiling salted water until just tender. Drain well and cool. Reserve several flowerettes for garnish. Top remaining broccoli flowerettes and stems with weight for 30 minutes to extract excess water. Pat dry. Purée broccoli in food processor until very smooth, about 2 minutes. Transfer to bowl. Beat in cream and egg. Salt and pepper to taste. Brush 4-6 ½-cup molds with butter. Divide mousse among prepared molds, spreading evenly. Arrange molds in roasting pan. Pour in enough simmering water to come halfway up sides of molds. Bake at 350 degrees until firm, about 45 minutes. Cool in molds 20 minutes.

LEMON BUTTER SAUCE
1	**tablespoon lemon juice**
1	**tablespoon heavy cream**
1	**cup (2 sticks) well-chilled unsalted butter, cut into small pieces**
	Salt and freshly ground pepper to taste

Boil lemon juice in small heavy saucepan until reduced to glaze. Reduce heat to low and whisk in cream. Whisk in butter, 1 tablespoon at a time. Salt and pepper to taste. Unmold mousses onto plates. Surround with some of the sauce. Garnish with reserved broccoli flowerettes. Serve immediately, passing remaining sauce separately.

BROCCOLI-ONION CASSEROLE

PREPARATION TIME: *1 hour*
YIELD: *6 servings*

1 **pound broccoli (or 1 10-ounce package frozen broccoli)**	Cook broccoli until tender. Cut into 1-inch pieces. Set aside. Cook onions in boiling salted water until tender. Drain and set aside. In small saucepan, melt butter. Blend in flour, salt and pepper. Add milk and cook, stirring until thick and bubbly. Reduce heat. Blend in cream cheese until smooth. Place vegetables in 1½-quart casserole. Pour cream sauce over and mix lightly. Top with cheese. Before baking, mix bread crumbs with butter and sprinkle on casserole. Bake at 350 degrees, for 30 minutes.
2 **cups whole pearl onions**	
2 **tablespoons butter**	
2 **tablespoons flour**	
¼ **teaspoon salt**	
⅛ **teaspoon pepper**	
1 **cup milk**	
1 **3-ounce package cream cheese**	
½ **cup shredded sharp Cheddar cheese**	
⅓ **cup bread crumbs**	
2 **tablespoons butter, softened**	

BOURBON BROCCOLI

PREPARATION TIME: *10-15 minutes*
YIELD: *4 servings*

1 **pound broccoli**	Cut broccoli into flowerettes. Cut stems diagonally into ½-inch pieces. In small bowl, mix together bourbon, water, sugar and salt. In wok or large skillet, stir-fry broccoli over high heat for about 3 minutes. Add bourbon sauce. Reduce heat. Cover and cook 5-6 minutes, stirring occasionally.
¼ **cup bourbon**	
¼ **cup water**	
1 **teaspoon sugar**	
⅛ **teaspoon salt**	
2 **tablespoons oil**	

LEMON BROCCOLI

PREPARATION TIME: *30-35 minutes*
YIELD: *6-8 servings*

1½ pounds broccoli

SAUCE
1 teaspoon grated lemon peel

½ teaspoon ginger

¼ teaspoon salt

⅓ cup milk

1 tablespoon lemon juice

2 3-ounce packages cream cheese, softened

GARNISH
1 tablespoon butter

½ cup slivered almonds

Cook broccoli until just tender. Drain. In double boiler, combine sauce ingredients. Heat and stir with whisk until smooth and creamy.

In a small skillet, sauté almonds in butter until light golden brown. Pour sauce over broccoli and garnish with almonds.

Prepare sauce at the last minute to avoid curdling.

PURPLE CABBAGE

PREPARATION TIME: *30 minutes*
YIELD: *12 servings*

4 slices bacon

1 onion, chopped

1 apple, chopped but not peeled

1 small green cabbage, chopped

1 large red cabbage, chopped

¼ cup wine vinegar

2 teaspoons sugar

2 tablespoons water

2 tablespoons flour

Salt and pepper to taste

Fry bacon until crisp. Add onion and apple and fry until tender. Add cabbages, vinegar, sugar and water. Steam until cabbage is tender, about 10 minutes. Stir in flour and cook 10 minutes longer. Salt and pepper to taste.

Excellent with pork roasts or Polish sausage.

MARINATED CAULIFLOWER

PREPARATION TIME: *1 hour plus chilling time*
YIELD: *4-6 servings*

1 head cauliflower
2 tablespoons white wine vinegar (or white wine tarragon vinegar)
2 tablespoons oil
1 clove garlic, minced
½ cup sour cream
2 tablespoons lemon juice
1 teaspoon Dijon mustard
1 tablespoon minced parsley
Salt and pepper to taste
1 tablespoon minced parsley
1 teaspoon grated lemon peel (optional)

Cook cauliflower and cut into pieces. Whisk vinegar, oil and garlic together. Pour over warm cauliflower and chill about 1 hour. In a small bowl, mix sour cream, lemon juice, mustard, 1 tablespoon parsley, salt and pepper. Set aside. Drain cauliflower. Toss gently with sour cream mixture and sprinkle with 1 tablespoon parsley and lemon peel. Chill at least 1 hour before serving.

CELERY AND MUSHROOM BAKE

PREPARATION TIME: *1 hour, 10 minutes*
YIELD: *4-6 servings*

4 cups diced celery
½ pound mushrooms, sliced
2 tablespoons minced onion
Salt and pepper to taste
4 tablespoons butter, melted
¼ cup slivered almonds, toasted

Add green bell pepper for variety.

Place celery and mushrooms on large piece of aluminum foil. Sprinkle with onion, salt and pepper. Drizzle with butter. Close foil tightly. Bake at 400 degrees for 1 hour. Sprinkle with almonds before serving.

COLD GLAZED CARROTS

PREPARATION TIME: *30 minutes plus chilling time*
YIELD: *10 servings*

3 **pounds carrots**
1 **8-ounce can jellied cranberry sauce**
¼ **cup water**
¼ **cup brown sugar**
4 **teaspoons Grand Marnier**

Peel and cut carrots julienne style. Cook until just tender. Rinse in cold water. In small saucepan, combine cranberry sauce, water and brown sugar. Cook over low heat until syrupy. Remove from heat. Add liqueur. Pour sauce over carrots and toss gently. Chill carrots in sauce at least 2 hours, preferably overnight.

Keeps well in refrigerator for up to 10 days.

GINGERED CARROTS

PREPARATION TIME: *25-30 minutes*
YIELD: *8 servings*

2 **pounds carrots**
2 **tablespoons peeled and finely grated ginger root (or 1½ teaspoons ground ginger)**
6 **tablespoons butter**
2 **tablespoons honey**
Salt and pepper to taste

Cut carrots diagonally into ⅛-inch slices. Cook until just tender. Drain. In large skillet, cook ginger root in butter over moderate heat, stirring for 1 minute. Stir in honey. Add carrots, tossing to coat. Cook 1-2 minutes. Salt and pepper to taste.

HERBED CARROTS

PREPARATION TIME: *30-45 minutes*
YIELD: *4 servings*

1	pound carrots, sliced
4	tablespoons butter
½	cup chicken broth
2	teaspoons minced fresh parsley
2	teaspoons snipped fresh dill
	Salt and pepper to taste

Cook carrots until just tender. Drain. Rinse in cold water. In large skillet, melt butter. Add carrots and toss until well coated. Add broth. Cook mixture over moderate high heat, tossing until liquid is reduced to a glaze. Stir in parsley and dill. Salt and pepper to taste.

PICKLED CARROTS

PREPARATION TIME: *30 minutes plus chilling time*
YIELD: *10 servings*

8	carrots
¼	cup sugar
¾	cup water
¾	cup vinegar
1	tablespoon mustard seeds
1	stick cinnamon, broken into pieces
3	whole cloves

Quarter carrots lengthwise and cut into 3-inch lengths. Cook carrots until just tender. Drain and cover with cold water. In medium saucepan, combine sugar, water, vinegar and spices. Bring to a boil and simmer for 10 minutes. Drain carrots and pack into a jar. Pour hot spice mixture over carrots. Let cool. Cover. Refrigerate 8 hours or overnight. Drain before serving.

TANGY CARROT BAKE

PREPARATION TIME: *45 minutes*
YIELD: *6-8 servings*

8	carrots, sliced
½	cup mayonnaise
1	tablespoon minced onion
1	tablespoon prepared horseradish
½	teaspoon salt
¼	teaspoon pepper
½	cup fine cracker crumbs
½	teaspoon paprika
¼	cup chopped fresh parsley

Cook carrots until just tender. Drain, saving ¼ cup of cooking liquid. Place carrots in greased oven-proof serving dish. In small bowl, combine reserved liquid with mayonnaise, onion, horseradish, salt and pepper. Spread over carrots. Sprinkle with cracker crumbs, paprika and parsley. Bake at 375 degrees, uncovered, for 15-20 minutes.

SUMMERTIME CUCUMBERS

PREPARATION TIME: *45 minutes*
YIELD: *6-8 servings*

⅔	cup vinegar
3	tablespoons sugar
½	teaspoon salt
½	teaspoon dill weed
2	cucumbers, strip peeled and thinly sliced
½	Bermuda onion, thinly sliced

In sealable container, mix vinegar, sugar, salt and dill. Add cucumber and onion. Seal container and turn upside down several times to mix. Place in freezer for 30 minutes. Remove from freezer and store in refrigerator until serving time.

EGGPLANT ÉLÉGANTE

PREPARATION TIME: *30-45 minutes*
YIELD: *8 servings*

1	**eggplant**
1	**teaspoon salt**
½	**teaspoon pepper**
3	**tablespoons butter**
3	**tablespoons oil**
1	**cup chopped onion**
2	**cloves garlic, minced**
2	**cups peeled and chopped tomatoes (about 3 tomatoes)**
⅛	**teaspoon thyme, basil or sage**
¼	**cup chopped parsley**
½	**cup bread crumbs**
1	**cup grated Swiss or Gruyère cheese**

Peel eggplant. Cut into 8 even slices. Trim to make identical rounds. Save trimmings. Place eggplant slices in well-oiled 9 x 13-inch oven-proof dish. Sprinkle with salt and pepper. Broil until soft, about 5 minutes. In medium saucepan, melt butter with oil. Sauté onion and garlic until golden. Add tomatoes and eggplant trimmings. Cook until thick. Stir in herb, parsley and crumbs. Pour over eggplant slices. Cover with cheese. Bake at 350 degrees until cheese melts, about 7 minutes.

LAYERED MUSHROOM BAKE

PREPARATION TIME: *1 hour, 15 minutes*
YIELD: *8-10 servings*

1½	**pounds mushrooms, sliced**
2	**6-ounce cans sliced black olives**
¼	**pound Cheddar cheese, grated**
2	**tablespoons flour**
1½	**teaspoons salt**
⅛	**teaspoon pepper**
½	**cup milk**
1	**cup seasoned bread crumbs (or crushed seasoned croutons)**

In an 8-inch square baking dish, layer half of mushrooms, black olives and cheese. Repeat layering with remaining mushrooms, olives and cheese. In a small bowl, mix together flour, salt, pepper and milk. Pour mixture over casserole. Top with seasoned bread crumbs. Bake at 350 degrees for 30 minutes.

STUFFED MUSHROOMS

PREPARATION TIME: *45 minutes*
YIELD: *4-6 servings*

12	**large mushrooms**
4	**tablespoons butter**
2	**scallions, chopped**
½	**clove garlic, minced**
2	**medium fresh tomatoes (or 4 canned tomatoes), diced**
	Salt and pepper to taste
½	**cup bread crumbs**

Clean mushrooms. Remove stems. Reserve caps and set aside. Finely chop stems. In a large skillet, melt butter. Sauté stems, scallions and garlic for 5 minutes. Add tomatoes. Salt and pepper to taste. Remove from heat. Stir in bread crumbs. Fill mushroom caps with mixture. Place on cookie sheet and broil until golden brown, about 10 minutes.

HONEY BAKED ONIONS

PREPARATION TIME: *1 hour*
YIELD: *4-6 servings*

⅓	**cup honey**
4	**tablespoons butter**
½	**teaspoon salt**
6	**large onions, sliced**
1	**tablespoon lemon juice**
4	**drops Tabasco sauce**

In small saucepan, heat honey, butter and salt. Arrange onion slices in greased 9 x 13-inch baking dish. Sprinkle with lemon juice and Tabasco sauce. Pour honey-butter mixture evenly over onions. Bake at 425 degrees for 45 minutes or until fork tender and golden brown in color.

PETITS POIS PURÉE

PREPARATION TIME: *15 minutes*
YIELD: *6 servings*

3	**10-ounce packages frozen peas, thawed**
2	**tablespoons butter**
½	**cup heavy cream**
	Salt and pepper to taste

Purée peas in blender or food processor. Melt butter in medium skillet. Add peas and cream. Bring to boil and continue cooking 2 minutes longer. Season to taste.

Especially attractive when served in tomato shells.

HERBED POTATO CRISPS

PREPARATION TIME: *30 minutes*
YIELD: *4-6 servings*

4	**medium potatoes, cut into ¾-inch cubes**
1	**tablespoon oil**
1	**tablespoon butter**
1	**tablespoon butter**
⅛	**teaspoon tarragon, or mixed herbs**
3	**tablespoons minced fresh parsley**

In large skillet, heat oil with 1 tablespoon butter. Dry potatoes. Sauté over medium heat, tossing frequently, until browned and tender, about 15 minutes. Add remaining butter, herbs and parsley. Toss mixture over high heat to crisp.

MASHED POTATO SOUFFLÉ

PREPARATION TIME: *1 hour, 30 minutes*
YIELD: *6 servings*

4-6 potatoes, peeled

1 8-ounce package cream cheese

1 egg

1 cup light cream

Salt and pepper to taste

Tabasco sauce to taste

¼ cup chopped scallions

Boil potatoes until tender. Drain. While still hot, whip potatoes with cream cheese, egg and cream. Season to taste with salt, pepper and Tabasco sauce. Fold in scallions. Pour into buttered casserole or soufflé dish, leaving 2-3 inches at the top for "puffing." Bake at 350 degrees for 45 minutes.

Soufflé can be assembled and refrigerated until baking time.

MINTED NEW POTATOES

PREPARATION TIME: *25-30 minutes*
YIELD: *6 servings*

2 pounds new potatoes

4 tablespoons butter, melted

1 tablespoon minced fresh mint leaves

Salt to taste

Steam potatoes, partially covered, for 6 to 10 minutes. Transfer carefully to heated serving dish. Drizzle with melted butter. Sprinkle with mint. Salt to taste.

POTATOES AND ARTICHOKES

PREPARATION TIME: *1 hour, 30 minutes*
YIELD: *4-6 servings*

2 tablespoons butter

½ cup chopped onion

1 small clove garlic, minced

3 baking potatoes, peeled and very thinly sliced

1 cup heavy cream

⅓ cup milk

½ teaspoon bouillon granules

1 teaspoon salt

¼ teaspoon pepper

¼ teaspoon crumbled thyme leaves

1 8-ounce jar marinated artichoke hearts, drained and cut into quarters

1 lemon

Butter bottom and sides of an 8-inch square pan. Sprinkle onion and garlic in pan. Layer potatoes. In a small bowl, mix cream, milk and spices. Pour over potatoes. Layer on artichoke hearts and squeeze lemon juice over top. Bake at 350 degrees until top is browned, about 1 hour.

Can be cooked in microwave on high power for 25 minutes.

WORCESTERSHIRE POTATOES

PREPARATION TIME: *30 minutes*
YIELD: *6 servings*

6 medium potatoes

½ cup butter

2 teaspoons Worcestershire sauce

1 teaspoon salt

¼ teaspoon paprika

Cut potatoes into julienne strips. Boil in lightly salted water for 5 minutes. Drain. Cover cookie sheet with aluminum foil and spread with potatoes. Melt butter in small saucepan. Stir in Worcestershire sauce, salt and paprika. Heat thoroughly. Brush potatoes with sauce. Bake at 375 degrees until brown and crisp, about 15-20 minutes.

HONEY-STUFFED SWEET POTATOES

PREPARATION TIME: *1 hour, 30 minutes*
YIELD: *6 servings*

6	sweet potatoes
4	tablespoons butter
¼	cup heavy cream
2	tablespoons honey
2	tablespoons dark rum
½	teaspoon cardamon
	Salt and pepper to taste
½	cup chopped walnuts

Bake potatoes at 425 degrees for 20 minutes. Prick with fork and bake 25 minutes longer, or until tender. Remove potatoes from oven. Cut each potato lengthwise in a ⅓:⅔ proportion. Scoop out pulp into medium bowl, being careful not to puncture shells. Reserve the larger shell from each potato. Mash pulp with butter, cream, honey, rum and seasonings. Spoon into reserved shells. Top with nuts. Bake at 450 degrees for 10 minutes.

SPAGHETTI SQUASH PRIMAVERA

PREPARATION TIME: *1 hour, 30 minutes*
YIELD: *8 servings*

1	spaghetti squash
1	10-ounce package frozen spinach (or 2 bunches fresh spinach)
¼	cup milk
4	tablespoons butter
1	teaspoon basil
2	cloves garlic, minced
	Salt and pepper to taste
1	cup sliced fresh mushrooms
1	tablespoon butter
1-2	tablespoons butter, melted
½	cup grated Cheddar cheese
¼	cup grated Parmesan cheese

Boil squash whole for 1 hour. Cook spinach according to package directions. Drain well. Set aside. In small saucepan, heat, but do not boil, milk, 4 tablespoons butter, basil, garlic, salt and pepper to taste. Keep warm. In small skillet, sauté mushrooms in 1 tablespoon butter. Set aside. Melt 2 tablespoons butter in large saucepan over low heat. Split squash in half lengthwise and remove seeds. Scoop out pulp into large saucepan. Add spinach, milk mixture and mushrooms. Toss lightly. Add cheeses. Toss until well mixed and cheeses are melted.

SPAGHETTI SQUASH WITH ITALIAN SAUSAGE

PREPARATION TIME: *1 hour*
YIELD: *4-6 servings*

1	medium-size spaghetti squash
½	pound sweet Italian sausage
½	pound hot Italian sausage
1	15-ounce can tomato sauce
1	clove garlic, minced
2	teaspoons Italian seasoning
⅛	teaspoon pepper
½	teaspoon Tabasco sauce
1	tablespoon olive oil
1	cup grated zucchini (1 medium zucchini)
¾	cup grated Mozzarella cheese
¾	cup grated Cheddar cheese
¼	cup grated Parmesan cheese

Cut squash in half, lengthwise. Discard seeds. Cook squash. Conventional oven: Place squash, cut side down, in about 2 inches of water in large pan. Cover and simmer until tender, for about 20 minutes. Microwave oven: Place small amount of water in bottom of pan and place squash cut side up. Cover with plastic wrap and cook on high power until tender, about 10 minutes.

While squash is cooking, prepare sauce. Remove casings from sausages and sauté in dry skillet. Drain off fat. Add tomato sauce, garlic, Italian seasoning, pepper and Tabasco sauce. Simmer several minutes. When squash is done, remove strands from shell and place strands in large bowl. Place squash shells in a baking dish just large enough to hold them upright. Toss the squash strands with olive oil. Add zucchini, Mozzarella cheese, Cheddar cheese and sauce. Mix well. Spoon mixture back into shells and top with Parmesan cheese. Bake at 350 degrees for 20-30 minutes.

SQUASH SOUFFLÉ

PREPARATION TIME: *45 minutes*
YIELD: *6 servings*

2	**egg whites**
2	**10-ounce packages frozen winter squash, thawed**
3	**tablespoons butter, melted**
⅓	**cup brown sugar**
¾	**teaspoon salt**
⅛	**teaspoon cinnamon**
⅛	**teaspoon nutmeg**
⅛	**teaspoon ginger**
2	**egg yolks**
2	**tablespoons brandy**
½	**cup chopped nuts**

Beat egg whites until stiff. Set aside. Mix all remaining ingredients together. Fold in beaten egg whites. Bake in a 9 x 13-inch greased casserole at 350 degress for 35 minutes.

ORANGE-FLAVORED HOLLANDAISE SAUCE

PREPARATION TIME: *10 minutes*
YIELD: *1 cup*

3	**egg yolks**
1	**tablespoon fresh-squeezed lemon juice**
1	**tablespoon fresh-squeezed orange juice**
¼	**teaspoon salt**
	Red pepper (cayenne) to taste
½	**cup butter**
1	**teaspoon grated orange peel**
1	**tablespoon orange juice**

Combine egg yolks, lemon juice, 1 tablespoon orange juice, salt and pepper in blender. Blend for a few seconds. Heat butter until foamy. Turn blender to high speed and slowly pour in hot butter. Scrape sides of blender with spatula. Add orange peel and remaining tablespoon orange juice. Blend for a few seconds.

This light sauce is simple to make, tastes delicious and looks elegant.

SPINACH-ARTICHOKE CASSEROLE

PREPARATION TIME: *1 hour*
YIELD: *8 servings*

2	**10-ounce packages frozen, chopped spinach, thawed**
1	**14¾-ounce jar marinated artichoke hearts, drained**
½	**teaspoon salt**
1	**8-ounce package cream cheese, softened**
2	**tablespoons butter, softened**
4	**tablespoons milk**
1	**teaspoon lemon juice**
	Pepper to taste
½	**cup grated Parmesan cheese**

Squeeze spinach until dry. Mix artichoke hearts, spinach, salt, cream cheese, butter, milk and lemon juice. Pour into 9 x 13-inch greased baking dish. Sprinkle with pepper to taste and Parmesan cheese. Bake at 350 degrees for 30-40 minutes.

SPINACH RING WITH MUSHROOM SAUCE

PREPARATION TIME: *1 hour, 15 minutes*
YIELD: *6-8 servings*

SPINACH RING
3	10-ounce packages frozen, chopped spinach
1	pound bulk pork sausage
3	eggs
2	teaspoons onion juice
	Salt and pepper to taste

Cook spinach. Drain well. Cook sausage. Drain well. Mix spinach and sausage with remaining ingredients. Pour into greased large ring mold. Place mold in pan of 1-inch-deep water. Bake at 350 degrees for 40 minutes.

MUSHROOM SAUCE
½	cup sliced mushrooms
1	tablespoon butter
2	tablespoons butter
2	tablespoons flour
1	cup chicken broth
2	tablespoons sherry
	Salt and pepper to taste

Sauté mushrooms in 1 tablespoon butter. Set aside. Melt 2 tablespoons butter in saucepan. Stir in flour. Whisk in broth and cook until thick. Add sherry. Salt and pepper to taste. Lightly fold in mushrooms. Unmold spinach ring onto serving dish. Serve sauce on the side.

Great brunch or luncheon entrée.

CHEDDAR TOMATOES

PREPARATION TIME: *1 hour*
YIELD: *6 servings*

1½	pounds tomatoes
2	tablespoons butter
2	tablespoons sherry
	Salt and pepper to taste
2	tablespoons heavy cream
3	tablespoons grated Cheddar cheese
2-3	tablespoons minced parsley

Peel and thinly slice tomatoes. Divide slices among 6 buttered 4-inch gratin dishes. Add 1 teaspoon sherry to each dish. Sprinkle tomatoes with salt and pepper. Bake at 300 degrees for 30 minutes. To each dish, add 2 teaspoons cream and 3 teaspoons cheese. Bake for 15 minutes more. Garnish with parsley.

VEGETABLE KABOBS WITH PATIO SAUCE

PREPARATION TIME: *30 minutes*
YIELD: *6-8 servings*

PATIO SAUCE

| 1 | **8-ounce can tomato sauce** |

| 2 | **tablespoons molasses** |

| 1 | **tablespoon cider vinegar** |

| ⅛ | **teaspoon dried tarragon leaves** |

| ⅛ | **teaspoon dry mustard** |

In a small bowl, combine tomato sauce, molasses, vinegar, tarragon and mustard. Mix well.

SUGGESTED VEGETABLES

small whole onions, parboiled

zucchini, cut into ½-inch slices, blanched

eggplant, cut into 1-inch cubes, blanched

tomato wedges or cherry tomatoes

corn on the cob, cut into 2-inch pieces

large mushrooms

green bell peppers, cut into sixths

Place vegetables on 8-inch skewers. Brush with sauce and broil or grill 3 minutes on each side.

VEGETABLE MÉLANGE

PREPARATION TIME: *1 hour, 30 minutes*
YIELD: *8-10 servings*

2	**medium carrots, thinly sliced**
2	**small potatoes, cubed**
4	**medium tomatoes, quartered**
1	**small head cauliflower, separated**
½	**green bell pepper, julienned**
½	**red bell pepper, julienned**
½	**10-ounce package frozen peas, thawed**
1	**cup fresh green beans**
1	**celery stalk, sliced**
3	**small zucchini, sliced**
1	**cup beef or chicken broth**
1	**cup olive oil**
½	**bay leaf**
¼	**teaspoon tarragon**
	Salt and pepper to taste

Put all vegetables in ungreased, shallow, 11 x 13-inch dish. Heat broth, oil, garlic and spices to boiling. Pour over vegetables. Cover with heavy foil. Bake at 350 degrees until just tender, about 1 hour.

Vary types of vegetables to suit season.

ZUCCHINI CHEESE SOUFFLÉ

PREPARATION TIME: *1 hour, 30 minutes*
YIELD: *4 servings*

½ **pound zucchini, grated**

¼ **teaspoon salt**

2-4 **tablespoons butter**

2 **tablespoons grated Parmesan cheese**

3 **tablespoons butter**

3 **tablespoons flour**

¾ **cup scalded milk**

¼ **cup minced onion**

2 **tablespoons butter**

½ **cup grated Swiss cheese**

¼ **cup grated Parmesan cheese**

Nutmeg, salt and pepper to taste

5 **egg whites**

¼ **teaspoon cream of tartar**

⅛ **teaspoon salt**

1 **tablespoon grated Parmesan cheese**

In colander, toss zucchini with ¼ teaspoon salt and let stand for 30 minutes. Squeeze zucchini in a tea towel, removing as much water as possible. Fit a well-buttered 1-quart soufflé dish with a 3-inch-wide collar of wax paper, doubled and buttered to form a standing collar extending 2 inches above the rim. Sprinkle casserole and collar with 2 tablespoons Parmesan cheese. In saucepan, melt 3 tablespoons butter. Stir in flour and cook roux over low heat, stirring for 3 minutes. Remove pan from heat and add milk, whisking vigorously until thick and smooth. Transfer sauce to large bowl. In medium skillet, sauté onion in 2 tablespoons butter for 2 minutes. Add zucchini and cook mixture for 2 minutes. Add zucchini mixture to sauce. Stir in cheeses. Add nutmeg, salt and pepper to taste. Combine well. In another bowl, beat 5 egg whites until foamy. Add cream of tartar and salt. Continue to beat until stiff peaks form. Fold whites gently but thoroughly into zucchini mixture. Pour entire mixture into prepared soufflé dish. Sprinkle top with 1 tablespoon Parmesan cheese. Bake at 375 degrees until puffed and golden, about 30 minutes.

ZUCCHINI-MUSHROOM FRITTATA

PREPARATION TIME: *1½ hours*
YIELD: *6-8 servings*

2 medium zucchini, chopped

½ pound mushrooms, chopped

1 medium green bell pepper, chopped

1 medium onion, chopped

1 clove garlic, minced

3 tablespoons oil

6 eggs

¼ cup light cream

2 8-ounce packages cream cheese, diced

2 cups stale white bread, cubed (crusts removed)

1½ cups grated Cheddar cheese

Salt and pepper to taste

In large skillet, sauté zucchini, mushrooms, green bell pepper, onion and garlic in oil until vegetables are softened, about 5 minutes. Remove pan from heat and let mixture cool. In large bowl, beat eggs with cream. Add cream cheese, bread, Cheddar cheese, vegetable mixture, salt and pepper. Mix well. Pour mixture into greased 10-inch spring form pan and bake at 350 degrees until browned and set, about 55 minutes. Let stand 10 minutes. Carefully remove sides of pan and, with broad spatulas, transfer frittata to heated serving plate. Serve warm, cut into wedges.

HOMEMADE NOODLES WITH POPPY SEEDS

PREPARATION TIME: *1 hour, 30 minutes*
YIELD: *6-8 servings*

4	**eggs**
1	**teaspoon salt**
2½-3	**cups flour**
½	**cup butter**
1	**small onion, chopped**
2	**teaspoons poppy seeds**
1	**tablespoon oil**

In large bowl, beat eggs with salt. Beat in 1 cup flour. Continue adding small amount of flour. When no longer able to mix in flour, turn dough onto floured surface and knead in additional flour until dough is smooth and no longer sticky, about 10 minutes. Cover dough with a bowl and let rest 1 hour. Divide dough into fourths. With rolling pin, roll one portion into a rectangle ⅛-inch thick. Dust with flour and tightly roll up, jelly-roll fashion. With sharp knife, cut into ⅛-inch slices. Uncurl slices and set aside. Repeat process with remaining dough. In small saucepan, melt butter and sauté onions until soft. Add poppy seeds. Stir and set aside. Add oil to large pot of boiling water. Cook noodles until tender. Drain and toss with poppy seed mixture.

Any herb may be substituted for poppy seeds.

PASTA WITH SAGE SAUCE

PREPARATION TIME: *20 minutes*
YIELD: *6-8 servings*

½	**cup light cream**
½	**teaspoon sage**
½	**cup butter**
1	**small bunch broccoli, flowerettes only**
1	**8-ounce package pasta**
½	**cup grated Parmesan cheese**
	Ground pepper to taste
¾	**cup grated Parmesan cheese**

Heat cream with sage over low heat to reduce liquid slightly, about 5 minutes. Add butter. When melted, add broccoli. Cover and cook. While preparing broccoli, cook pasta until al dente. Drain and immediately toss with sauce, ½ cup Parmesan and pepper. Pass remaining Parmesan cheese.

COGNAC RICE

PREPARATION TIME: *1 hour, 45 minutes*
YIELD: *4 servings*

½	**cup golden raisins**
½	**cup cognac**
1	**onion, chopped**
3	**tablespoons butter, melted**
1	**cup rice**
2½	**cups chicken broth**
½	**cup shelled pistachios**
2	**tablespoons minced parsley**
⅛	**teaspoon salt**
¼	**teaspoon black pepper**

Soak raisins in cognac for 1 hour. Sauté onions in butter until softened. Add raisins with cognac. Stir in rice and brown slightly. Add broth and bring to a boil. Reduce heat and simmer for 25 minutes or until rice is done. Fluff and toss with pistachios, parsley, salt and pepper.

RISOTTO À LA SUISSE

PREPARATION TIME: *30 minutes*
YIELD: *4 servings*

1	**small onion, finely chopped**
4	**tablespoons butter**
½	**cup white wine**
1½	**cups chicken broth**
	Freshly ground black pepper to taste
1	**cup long grain rice**
4	**ounces Swiss cheese, grated**
2	**tablespoons chives**

In small, heavy saucepan, sauté onion in butter until golden brown. Add wine, broth and pepper. Bring to a boil. Add rice. Continue boiling for 5 minutes, stirring well. Cover saucepan. Reduce heat and simmer 15 minutes. Remove from heat. Fold in cheese. Cover and let stand until cheese has melted. Sprinkle with chives. Stir.

WILD RICE CASSEROLE

PREPARATION TIME: *1 hour*
YIELD: *8 servings*

1	**6-ounce package wild and long grain rice**
6	**slices bacon**
1	**large onion, chopped**
3	**large celery stalks, chopped**
½	**pound fresh mushrooms, sliced**
½	**cup blanched, slivered almonds**
½	**teaspoon oregano**
⅛	**teaspoon salt**
¼	**teaspoon pepper**
1¼	**cups chicken broth**

Cook rice. Fry bacon. Drain and crumble. In same skillet, sauté onions, celery and mushrooms until soft. Place rice, bacon, vegetables, nuts and seasonings in buttered casserole. Mix lightly. Add broth and toss. Bake at 350 degrees, uncovered, for 30 minutes.

BREADS

Pleasures from the Oven

BREAD STICKS

PREPARATION TIME: *30 minutes*
YIELD: *18 bread sticks*

4 tablespoons butter

1¼ cups flour

2 teaspoons sugar

2 teaspoons baking powder

1 teaspoon salt

⅔ cup milk

Melt butter in 9 x 9 x 2-inch oven-proof pan at 450 degrees for about 3 minutes. Mix flour, sugar, baking powder, salt and milk and stir until mixed well. Turn dough onto well floured board. Roll dough around and coat with flour. Knead lightly 10 times. Shape into an 8-inch square. Cut dough in half. Cut each half into 9 4-inch strips. Put strips in pan and coat both sides with butter. Arrange strips close together in pan. Bake at 450 degrees until golden brown, about 15 minutes.

FOOLPROOF FRENCH BREAD

PREPARATION TIME: *6 hours*
YIELD: *1 loaf*

4 cups white flour

1 tablespoon salt

2 tablespoons sugar

1 package dry yeast

2 cups lukewarm water

In large bowl, mix flour, salt and sugar together. In small bowl, dissolve yeast in water. Pour yeast mixture over other ingredients. Stir and mix. Cover bowl with plastic wrap and let rise 4 hours. Punch down, but do not knead. Place in greased soufflé dish. Cover and let rise 1 hour. Bake at 400 degrees for 1 hour. Bread may need to be covered during the last 15 minutes if it browns too quickly.

After removing from oven, brush loaf with butter to keep crust from getting too hard.

HOMEMADE DINNER ROLLS

PREPARATION TIME: *5 hours*
YIELD: *3 dozen*

1	package dry yeast
½	cup warm water
1	cup milk, scalded
2	tablespoons butter
2	tablespoons sugar
1	teaspoon salt
1	egg, beaten
3¼	cups flour
	Butter, melted

Mix yeast and water. Let stand 10 minutes. Mix milk, butter, sugar and salt together. Cool to luke warm. Combine both mixtures. Stir in egg and flour. Cover and let rise for 2 hours. Punch down and shape into 1-inch rolls. Place on greased baking sheet and let rise 2 more hours. Bake at 400 degrees for 12-15 minutes. Remove from oven and brush tops with butter.

OATMEAL BATTER BREAD

PREPARATION TIME: *2 hours*
YIELD: *1 loaf*

¾	cup boiling water
½	cup old-fashioned rolled oats
3	tablespoons shortening
¼	cup honey
1	teaspoon salt
¼	teaspoon apple pie spice
1	package dry yeast
½	teaspoon sugar
¼	cup warm water
1	egg, slightly beaten
1¼	cups flour
1½	cups flour

In medium bowl, stir together boiling water, oats, shortening, honey, salt and apple pie spice until well mixed. Cool. Mix yeast, sugar and warm water, stirring until dissolved. Add yeast mixture, egg and 1¼ cups flour to oatmeal mixture. Beat well. Gradually add remaining 1½ cups flour. Beat until batter is smooth. Spread batter into greased 9 x 5 x 3-inch loaf pan. Cover with towel and let rise 45 minutes. Bake at 375 degrees for 1 hour.

POTATO REFRIGERATOR DOUGH

PREPARATION TIME: *10 minutes plus rising time*
YIELD: *18 cups*

1 package dry yeast	Dissolve yeast in warm water. Add sugar, salt, eggs, shortening, mashed potatoes and 4 cups flour. Beat until smooth. Mix in enough flour to make dough easy to handle. Turn dough onto floured surface and knead for 5 minutes. Place in greased bowl. Cover tightly. Refrigerate at least 8 hours, but no longer than five days. Use as suggested in the following recipes.
1½ cups warm water	
½ cup sugar	
1½ teaspoons salt	
2 eggs	
⅓ cup shortening	
1 cup lukewarm mashed potatoes	
4 cups flour	
3-3½ cups flour	

Wonderfully versatile. Different rolls may be made fresh daily.

HAMBURGER BUNS

PREPARATION TIME: *20 minutes plus rising time*
YIELD: *12 buns*

6 cups Potato Refrigerator Dough	Divide dough into 12 equal parts. Shape into smooth balls. Place on greased baking sheet and let rise until double. Brush with butter and sprinkle with sesame seeds. Bake at 400 degrees for 10-15 minutes.
4 tablespoons butter, melted	
¼ cup sesame seeds	

PARKER HOUSE ROLLS

PREPARATION TIME: *30 minutes plus rising time*
YIELD: *20 rolls*

9 cups Potato Refrigerator Dough	Divide dough in half. On a floured surface, with rolling pin, roll each half into a 9 x 13-inch rectangle. Cut dough into 3-inch circles. Brush each circle with melted butter. Fold circle over so it overlaps other half of circle slightly. Press edges together. Place on greased baking sheet. Brush tops with melted butter. Let rise until double. Bake at 400 degrees for 15 minutes.
4 tablespoons butter, melted	

BRAIDED DINNER ROLLS

PREPARATION TIME: *30 minutes plus rising time*
YIELD: *6 rolls*

6 cups Potato Refrigerator Dough	Divide dough into 18 parts. Roll each part into a rope 7 inches long. Place three ropes together and braid gently and loosely. Do not stretch. Pinch ends to fasten. Place braids on greased baking sheet and let rise until double. Brush egg mixture over braids. Sprinkle braids with seeds. Bake at 375 degrees for 15 minutes.
1 egg, slightly beaten with 1 tablespoon water	
¼ cup sesame or poppy seeds	

CRESCENT ROLLS

PREPARATION TIME: *30 minutes plus rising time*
YIELD: *32 rolls*

9 cups Potato Refrigerator Dough

½ cup butter, melted

4 tablespoons butter, melted

Divide dough in half. On a floured surface, with a rolling pin, roll each half into a 12-inch circle. Brush with ½ cup melted butter. Cut circle into 16 wedges. Roll up each wedge starting at rounded edge. Place rolls on greased baking sheet. Curve ends slightly to form crescent. Brush with melted butter. Let rise until double. Bake at 400 degrees for 13-15 minutes.

Serve with Honey Butter, page 185.

SODA BREAD

PREPARATION TIME: *45 minutes*
YIELD: *1 loaf*

3½ cups flour

1 teaspoon baking soda

1 teaspoon salt

1 teaspoon honey

1 cup buttermilk or sour milk*

1 egg, beaten with 1 tablespoon water

Combine dry ingredients. Make a well in the center and add honey. Slowly add buttermilk, mixing into flour with fork. Add just enough milk to make mixture into dough. Knead briefly, then shape into round loaf. Place on greased baking sheet. Cut several times across entire top and down the side with a sharp knife. Brush top of loaf with egg and water mixture. Bake at 450 degrees for 15 minutes. Reduce heat to 350 degrees and bake 15 minutes more.

Try some chutney on the bread for a unique taste. For variety, add 1 teaspoon cinnamon or cardamon to dry ingredients. Sprinkle top of loaf with poppy or sesame seeds.

*Sour milk can be made by adding 1 tablespoon lemon juice to 1 cup milk and allowing mixture to stand for 5 minutes.

SWEDISH RYE BREAD

PREPARATION TIME: *4 hours, 30 minutes*
YIELD: *4 large loaves*

1 cup rye flour

½ teaspoon shortening

2 cups boiling water

1½ tablespoons orange peel, grated

1 tablespoon fennel

1½ cups light corn syrup

1 cup milk

1 cake yeast, dissolved in ¼ cup warm water

7 cups white flour

In large bowl, combine rye flour and shortening. Pour boiling water over mixture. Stir well. Add all remaining ingredients. Knead dough 10 minutes. Let rise, covered with damp cloth, until doubled, about 2 hours. Punch down. Divide dough into fourths and put each portion of dough into a well-greased 9 x 5 x 3-inch loaf pan. Cover and let rise approximately one hour. Bake at 350 degrees for 1½ hours.

BUTTERMILK CORNBREAD

PREPARATION TIME: *45 minutes*
YIELD: *16 servings*

1 cup flour

1 cup yellow cornmeal

½ cup sugar

2 eggs

1 cup buttermilk or sour milk*

½ teaspoon salt

½ teaspoon baking soda

1 tablespoon butter

Mix all ingredients together. Bake in buttered and floured 9½ x 9½ x 2-inch square pan at 400 degrees for 30 minutes.

See Soda Bread hint on page 166.
1 cup yogurt can be substituted for buttermilk.
Great with Hearty Chili, page 110.

DILLY CASSEROLE BREAD

PREPARATION TIME: *2 hours, 30 minutes*
YIELD: *1 round loaf*

1	**package dry yeast**
¼	**cup warm water**
1	**cup creamed cottage cheese, room temperature**
1	**tablespoon sugar**
1	**tablespoon minced onion**
1	**tablespoon butter**
2	**tablespoons dill seed**
1	**teaspoon salt**
¼	**teaspoon baking soda**
1	**egg**
2¼-2½	**cups flour**
1	**tablespoon butter, softened**
⅛	**teaspoon salt**

In a large bowl, soften yeast in water. Add cottage cheese, sugar, onion, butter, dill seed, salt, baking soda and egg. Mix well. Add flour to form a stiff dough. Cover and let rise in warm place until double in size, 50-60 minutes. Punch down and turn into a well greased 8-inch round casserole dish. Let rise again until double, 30-40 minutes. Bake at 350 degrees until golden brown, about 40-50 minutes. Immediately after removing from oven, brush with soft butter and sprinkle with salt.

GREEN ONION FLAT BREAD

PREPARATION TIME: *1 hour*
YIELD: *14 rounds*

2¼	**cups flour**
¾	**teaspoon salt**
1	**cup boiling water**
1	**teaspoon peanut oil**
¼	**teaspoon salt**
6	**large scallions, sliced**
1	**¼-inch slice fresh ginger, peeled and minced**
	Peanut oil

In food processor, combine flour and ¾ teaspoon salt. While machine is running, pour in water. Continue mixing for 40 seconds. Transfer dough to plastic bag and seal tightly. Let rest 30 minutes. Heat 1 teaspoon oil with ¼ teaspoon salt. Sauté scallions and ginger until tender. Cool. Turn dough onto well floured suface. Roll into a 14 x 16-inch rectangle. Spread scallion mixture evenly over dough. Roll up jelly-roll fashion. Cut into 14 1-inch slices. Flatten each slice on well floured surface. Flour the slices well. Roll each slice between wax paper to 5-inch circle. Pour remaining oil into large saucepan to depth of 1 inch. Heat to high. Add 1 circle of dough and fry until crisp, about 40 seconds per side. Drain on paper towels. Repeat with remaining dough. Cut into wedges and serve warm.

May be arranged on baking sheet and reheated at 300 degrees for 10-12 minutes.

HERB BREAD

PREPARATION TIME: *30 minutes*
YIELD: *6 servings*

1	**cup butter, softened**
½	**teaspoon garlic powder**
½	**teaspoon summer savory**
½	**teaspoon thyme**
2	**heaping tablespoons fresh parsley**
1	**loaf white bread, unsliced**

Mix butter, garlic powder, savory, thyme and parsley together. Cut crust off bread. Cut loaf lengthwise, and then crosswise 8 times. Spread all surfaces with herb butter. Put bread back together in a loaf.* Wrap in foil, leaving top open. Bake at 400 degrees for 15-20 minutes. Watch carefully to avoid burning.

Can be frozen at this point, tightly wrapped in foil. Thaw before baking.

SPINACH BREAD

PREPARATION TIME: *1 hour*
YIELD: *6-8 servings*

1½	**teaspoons minced onion**
½	**teaspoon garlic powder**
1½	**tablespoons olive oil**
2	**eggs, beaten**
¾	**cup grated Parmesan cheese**
2	**10-ounce packages frozen spinach, thawed**
1	**loaf frozen bread dough (or 6 cups Potato Refrigerator Dough)**
¾	**pound Mozzarella or Provolone cheese, thinly sliced**

Mix together onion, garlic powder, olive oil, egg and Parmesan. Squeeze out excess water from spinach. Roll bread dough out to ½-inch thickness. Spread cheese mixture over dough. Spread spinach over mixture. Cover with sliced cheese. Roll up jelly-roll fashion. Pinch edges and both ends. Bake on greased baking sheet at 350 degrees for 30-40 minutes. Slice and serve hot.

Serve with a tossed green salad and a glass of wine for a nice light meal.

BUTTERMILK COFFEE CRUMB CAKE

PREPARATION TIME: *1 hour*
YIELD: *8-10 servings*

CAKE
2½ cups flour

1 teaspoon cinnamon

1 teaspoon baking soda

1 teaspoon salt

½ cup butter

2 cups brown sugar, firmly packed

1 egg

1½ cups buttermilk

Mix flour, cinnamon, baking soda and salt together. Set aside. Cream together sugar and butter. Beat in egg. Add dry ingredients alternately with buttermilk. Pour batter into greased 9 x 13 x 2-inch pan.

CRUMB TOPPING
½ cup flour

½ cup brown sugar

4 tablespoons butter, softened

To prepare crumb topping, mix flour, brown sugar and butter together with fork or pastry cutter. Sprinkle on batter. Bake at 350 degrees for 45 minutes.

DUTCH CARROT BREAD

PREPARATION TIME: *1 hour, 30 minutes*
YIELD: *2 loaves*

2	**cups flour**
2	**teaspoons baking soda**
2	**teaspoons cinnamon**
½	**teaspoon salt**
1½	**cups sugar**
1½	**cups oil**
3	**eggs**
2	**teaspoons vanilla**
2	**cups grated carrots**
1	**cup nuts (optional)**
½	**cup raisins (optional)**

In large bowl, sift together flour, baking soda, cinnamon and salt. Make a well in the center and put in sugar, oil, eggs and vanilla. Beat until well blended. Fold in carrots, nuts and raisins. Turn mixture into two well greased and floured 9 x 5 x 3-inch loaf pans. Bake at 300 degrees until bread tests done, about 1 hour.

Great plain as well as with butter or cream cheese.
This is the first time this family treasure has been shared with anyone outside the family.

GLAZED BANANA BREAD

PREPARATION TIME: *1 hour, 30 minutes*
YIELD: *1 loaf*

BREAD

1	**cup sugar**
½	**cup butter, softened**
3	**ripe bananas, mashed**
2	**eggs**
2	**cups flour**
1	**teaspoon baking soda**
¼	**teaspoon salt**

Cream sugar and butter together. Add bananas and eggs. Beat well. Add flour, baking soda and salt. Mix well. Pour into greased 9 x 5 x 3-inch loaf pan. Bake at 350 degrees for 50-60 minutes.

GLAZE

1	**cup powdered sugar**
2	**teaspoons milk**

Mix together powdered sugar and milk to make a runny glaze. Drizzle over cooled bread.

Glaze makes this old stand-by special.

LEMON BREAD

PREPARATION TIME: *1 hour, 30 minutes*
YIELD: *2 loaves*

BREAD

2	cups sugar
1	cup butter
4	egg yolks
3¼	cups flour
1	teaspoon salt
2	teaspoons baking powder
1¼	cups milk
	Grated peel of 2 lemons
1	cup finely chopped nuts (optional)
4	egg whites

Cream sugar and butter together well. Beat in egg yolks. Sift dry ingredients together and add alternately with milk. Mix well. Add lemon peel and nuts. Beat egg whites until stiff and fold into batter. Grease and flour 2 9 x 5 x 3-inch loaf pans and divide batter between them. Bake at 350 degrees for 55-60 minutes.

TOPPING

	Juice of 2 lemons
½	cup sugar

Mix topping ingredients and spoon over bread. Leave bread in pans for 1 hour. Turn out of pans and cool completely on racks.

Good for breakfast or with a hearty soup.

PINEAPPLE ZUCCHINI BREAD

PREPARATION TIME: *1 hour, 45 minutes*
YIELD: *2 loaves*

3	eggs, beaten
1	cup oil
2	cups sugar
2	teaspoons vanilla
3	cups flour
2	teaspoons baking soda
1	teaspoon salt
½	teaspoon baking powder
1½	teaspoons cinnamon
¾	teaspoon nutmeg
2	cups coarsely shredded zucchini
1	8¼-ounce can crushed pineapple, drained
1	cup nuts
1	cup raisins

Mix eggs, oil, sugar and vanilla together. Mix dry ingredients and add to egg mixture. Stir in zucchini and pineapple. Add nuts and raisins and stir well. Divide between 2 greased and floured 9 x 5 x 3-inch loaf pans or pour into one greased and floured tube pan. Bake at 350 degrees for 1 hour for loaf pans, 1 hour, 15 minutes for tube pan. Cool 10 minutes and turn out on rack.

Delicious served with cream cheese.
Freezes well.

PUMPKIN-CHOCOLATE CHIP LOAF

PREPARATION TIME: *1 hour, 30 minutes*
YIELD: *2 loaves*

3	cups flour
3	cups sugar
2	teaspoons baking soda
½	teaspoon baking powder
1	teaspoon salt
1	teaspoon cloves
1	teaspoon allspice
1	teaspoon cinnamon
1	cup oil
4	eggs
⅔	cup water
2	cups canned pumpkin
1	12-ounce package chocolate chips

Mix together all ingredients except pumpkin and chocolate chips. Blend well. Add pumpkin to mixture and then fold in chocolate chips. Divide mixture between 2 greased and floured 9 x 5 x 3-inch loaf pans. Bake at 325 degrees for 1 hour, 15 minutes.

Very rich. Great with a dollop of whipped cream or a scoop of ice cream.

STRAWBERRY ALMOND BREAD

PREPARATION TIME: *1 hour, 30 minutes*
YIELD: *1 large or 3 small loaves*

2	eggs
½	cup oil
1	cup sugar
1	10-ounce package frozen strawberries, thawed and drained
1½	cups flour
1½	teaspoons cinnamon
½	teaspoon baking soda
¼	teaspoon salt
⅔	cup chopped almonds

In medium bowl, beat eggs until fluffy. Add oil, sugar and strawberries. In medium bowl, sift together flour, cinnamon, baking soda and salt. Stir in strawberry mixture. Mix until well blended. Stir in almonds. Grease and flour 1 large or 3 small loaf pans. Bake at 350 degrees for 1 hour, 10 minutes for large loaf, or 45 minutes for small loaves. Test for doneness with toothpick. Cool slightly and then turn onto racks to cool completely.

WALNUT BREAD

PREPARATION TIME: *1 hour, 15 minutes*
YIELD: *1 loaf*

1	egg
1	cup sugar
1	cup sour cream
1	teaspoon vanilla
¾	teaspoon baking soda
¼	teaspoon salt
2	cups flour
1	cup chopped walnuts

Beat egg, sugar, sour cream and vanilla together. Add soda, salt and flour. Stir in walnuts. Pour into greased 9 x 5 x 3-inch loaf pan. Bake at 350 degrees for 1 hour.

Serve with Sweet Lemon Butter, page 185.

APPLESAUCE MUFFINS

PREPARATION TIME: *45 minutes*
YIELD: *12 muffins*

½ **cup margarine**

¾ **cup light brown sugar, lightly packed**

1 **egg**

1 **cup flour**

½ **teaspoon cinnamon**

1 **teaspoon baking powder**

¼ **teaspoon baking soda**

¼ **teaspoon salt**

¾ **cup applesauce**

½ **cup raisins**

1 **cup quick-cooking rolled oats**

½ **cup chopped nuts (optional)**

Cream margarine. Gradually add brown sugar and cream until light and fluffy. Add egg and beat well. Add flour, cinnamon, baking powder, baking soda and salt and mix well. Add applesauce to batter, stirring well. Add raisins, oatmeal and nuts. Mix well. Spoon into 12 muffin cups. Bake at 350 degrees for 25-30 minutes. Cool on rack.

EASY CINNAMON ROLLS

PREPARATION TIME: *3 hours*
YIELD: *24 rolls*

1½ cups lukewarm water

½ cup sugar

1½ teaspoons salt

2 packages dry yeast

½ cup lukewarm water

1 egg

1 cup shortening

6½-7 cups flour

2 tablespoons cinnamon

1 cup brown sugar, firmly packed

½ cup pecans

½ cup butter, melted

In large bowl, mix 1½ cups lukewarm water, sugar and salt together. In small bowl, dissolve yeast in ½ cup water. Stir into sugar-water mixture. Add egg and shortening. Mix in flour and knead until completely combined. Place in greased bowl and turn dough over to coat. Cover with damp cloth and let rise 2 hours. Combine cinnamon, brown sugar and nuts. On floured surface, roll dough into 9 x 13-inch rectangle. Brush with melted butter and sprinkle with brown sugar mixture. Roll up dough jelly-roll fashion. Cut into 1-inch slices and place in greased muffin cups. Cover pans with damp cloth and let rise 45 minutes. Bake at 375 degrees for 25-30 minutes.

MAPLE SPICE MUFFINS

PREPARATION TIME: *30 minutes*
YIELD: *30 muffins*

1½ **cups whole wheat flour**

1¼ **cups white flour**

½ **cup quick-cooking rolled oats**

2 **teaspoons baking powder**

2 **teaspoons cinnamon**

1 **teaspoon baking soda**

½ **teaspoon cloves**

2 **eggs, beaten**

1 **8-ounce carton plain yogurt**

1 **cup maple syrup**

½ **cup brown sugar**

½ **cup oil**

1 **cup chopped walnuts**

1 **banana, chopped**

2 **cups maple syrup**

In large bowl, stir together flours, oats, baking powder, cinnamon, baking soda and cloves. Add eggs, yogurt and syrup. Beat in brown sugar and oil. Add nuts and banana, stirring until just mixed. Spoon into greased or paper-lined muffin cups. Fill ⅔ full. Bake at 400 degrees for 15-20 minutes. While warm, drizzle with additional maple syrup. Serve warm.

MINI ORANGE MUFFINS

PREPARATION TIME: *45 minutes*
YIELD: *72 muffins*

MUFFINS
½ cup butter

1 cup sugar

2 eggs

2 cups flour

¼ teaspoon salt

1 teaspoon baking soda

1 cup buttermilk or sour milk*

Grated rind of 2 oranges

Cream butter and sugar. Beat in eggs, one at a time. Sift flour, salt and baking soda together. Add to creamed mixture alternately with buttermilk. Fold in orange rind. Bake in greased mini-muffin cups at 375 degrees for 15 minutes.

SAUCE
1 cup brown sugar

Juice of 1 orange

Cook brown sugar and orange juice over low heat until sugar dissolves. Dip warm muffins in sauce. Place on wire rack to cool.

These muffins are great for breakfast or brunch, lunch or dinner.
1 cup yogurt can be substituted for buttermilk.

*See Soda Bread hint on page 166.

BLINTZ CASSEROLE

PREPARATION TIME: *1 hour*
YIELD: *6-8 servings*

BATTER

½ **pound margarine, melted (2 cups)**

½ **cup sugar**

2 **eggs**

1 **cup sifted flour**

3 **teaspoons baking powder**

⅛ **teaspoon salt**

¼ **cup milk**

1 **teaspoon vanilla (or other flavored extract)**

Mix all batter ingredients by hand.

FILLING

1 **16-ounce container ricotta cheese**

2 **eggs**

¾ **cup sugar**

⅛ **teaspoon salt**

4 **tablespoons lemon juice**

1 **8-ounce package cream cheese, softened**

In another bowl, blend together ingredients for filling. Place half of batter in a greased 9 x 13-inch pan. Top with all of filling. Cover filling with remainder of batter. Bake at 300 degrees for 1½ hours.

Perfect for brunch.
Serve with fresh fruit, marmalade or blueberry syrup.

COGNAC FRENCH TOAST

PREPARATION TIME: *35 minutes plus overnight*
YIELD: *15-18 slices per loaf of bread*

3 **baguettes (long, thin French breads), unsliced**	Cut baguettes into 1½-inch slices. Dissolve sugar in cognac and water. Dip bread slices in mixture. Place on baking sheets. Cover and refrigerate overnight. When ready to cook, mix eggs, milk, vanilla and salt together. Dip slices in mixture. Place on buttered baking sheet. Bake at 350 degrees until golden brown, about 10 minutes on each side.
½ **cup sugar**	
2 **cups cognac**	
2 **cups water**	
12 **eggs**	
½ **cup milk**	
2 **teaspoons vanilla**	
½ **teaspoon salt**	

GOUGÈRES

PREPARATION TIME: *1 hour, 15 minutes*
YIELD: *7 popovers*

1 **cup milk**	Heat milk and butter in 2-quart saucepan. Add salt and pepper. Bring to a full boil. Add flour all at once. Stir over medium heat until mixture leaves sides of pan and forms a ball. Remove from heat. Add eggs, one at a time, stirring until smooth and well blended. Beat ½ of cheese into batter with a large spoon. Divide dough into 8 even balls. Reserving 1 ball, place remaining 7 balls close together on greased baking sheet. With remainder of dough, make small mounds on top of original mounds. Sprinkle each with remaining cheese. Bake at 375 degrees for 55 minutes.
4 **tablespoons butter**	
¼ **teaspoon salt**	
Pepper to taste	
1 **cup all-purpose flour, unsifted**	
4 **eggs**	
1 **cup shredded Swiss cheese**	

SOUFFLÉED PEAR PANCAKES

PREPARATION TIME: *30 minutes*
YIELD: *2 large pancakes*

¾	cup white wine
½	cup water
½	cup sugar
1	tablespoon lemon juice
2	firm pears, peeled, halved and cut into thick slices
¾	cup light cream
½	cup flour
⅛	teaspoon salt
3	egg yolks
2	tablespoons butter, melted
3	egg whites
⅛	teaspoon salt
⅛	teaspoon cream of tartar
1	tablespoon sugar
4	tablespoons butter
	Syrup

Combine wine, water, ½ cup sugar and lemon juice. Bring to a boil, stirring until sugar is dissolved. Add pears and simmer until just tender, 10-15 minutes. Transfer pear slices to a small bowl. Reduce syrup in pan to 1 cup and reserve. In large bowl, combine cream, flour and ⅛ teaspoon salt. Beat in egg yolks, one at a time. Add butter. In another bowl, beat egg whites with salt, cream of tartar, and sugar until stiff peaks form. Fold egg whites into batter. In 8-inch skillet, melt 2 tablespoons butter until bubbly. Add half of batter, spreading evenly with spatula. Cook pancake 3 minutes over moderate heat. Arrange half of pear slices over pancake and place under broiler until puffed and golden brown. Slide pancake onto serving plate. Repeat process with remaining batter, pears and butter. Serve with syrup.

Can be used as breakfast or dessert pancakes.

SWEDISH PANCAKES WITH FRUIT SAUCE

PREPARATION TIME: *1 hour*
YIELD: *36 pancakes, 2 cups fruit sauce*

PANCAKES
- 4 eggs, beaten until foamy
- 1 cup milk
- 1 cup flour
- ½ teaspoon salt
- 1 tablespoon sugar
- 4 tablespoons butter

Beat all pancake ingredients, except butter, until smooth. In large skillet, melt enough butter to lightly coat bottom. Use 2 tablespoons batter per pancake. Make each pancake very thin. Cook until batter sets and turn once. Serve warm.

FRUIT SAUCE
- 2 cups chopped fresh fruit
- ¾ cup water
- 1 tablespoon sugar
- Salt to taste
- 1 tablespoon cornstarch
- 1 tablespoon cold water
- 1 teaspoon lemon juice
- Sugar to taste

In medium skillet, mix together fruit, ¾ cup water, 1 tablespoon sugar and salt. Cook and stir over medium heat about 5 minutes. Do not overcook! In separate bowl, blend cornstarch and cold water. Stir cornstarch mixture into fruit. Cook and stir until thick and bubbly. Stir in lemon juice. Add extra sugar to taste. Cool slightly, but serve warm.

Pancakes can be frozen between sheets of wax paper and reheated in microwave.

HONEY BUTTER

PREPARATION TIME: *5 minutes*
YIELD: *¾ cup*

½ cup butter	Beat butter with egg yolk and vanilla. Gradually add honey. Beat until creamy.
1 egg yolk	
¼ teaspoon vanilla	
½ cup honey	

A delicious spread for croissants, rolls and warm, homemade bread!

SWEET LEMON BUTTER

PREPARATION TIME: *25 minutes*
YIELD: *2 cups*

½ cup butter	Melt butter in top of double boiler. Stir in lemon peel, juice, sugar and salt. Lightly beat whole eggs into egg yolks. Blend eggs into sugar mixture. Cook over boiling water, beating with whisk until thick and smooth, about 20 minutes. Cover and store in refrigerator.
Grated peel of 1 lemon	
½ cup freshly-squeezed lemon juice	
1½ cups sugar	
¼ teaspoon salt	
3 whole eggs	
3 egg yolks	

Sweet Lemon Butter makes a delicious dip for fresh strawberries or a zippy spread for nut breads.

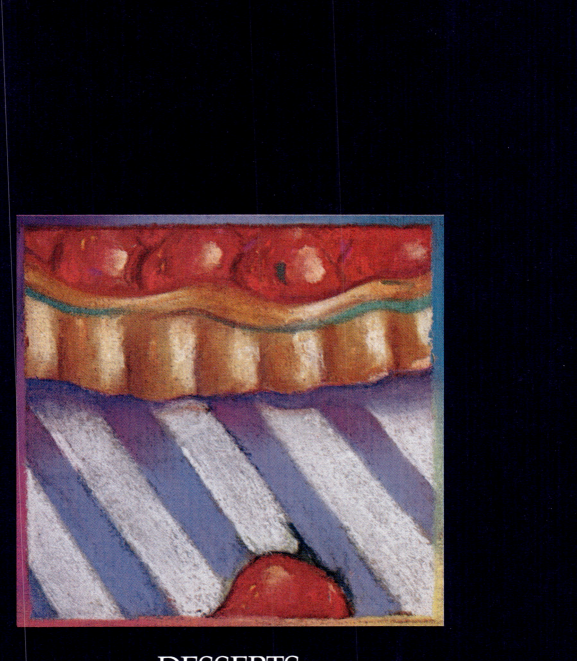

DESSERTS

Sweet Pleasures

ALMOND ROCA

PREPARATION TIME: *40 minutes*
YIELD: *40 2 x 2-inch pieces*

1	**cup sugar**
¼	**cup water**
½	**cup slivered almonds**
1	**tablespoon light corn syrup**
1	**cup butter**
8	**ounces semi-sweet chocolate chips (1⅓ cups)**
¼	**cup chopped almonds**

In heavy saucepan, combine sugar, water, slivered almonds, corn syrup and butter. Bring mixture to a boil, stirring constantly, until it reaches 280 degrees on a candy thermometer (almonds will look lightly toasted). Pour onto a greased baking sheet and spread thin to reach all corners. Melt chocolate and spread over almond rocca. Sprinkle chopped almonds over the top and cool completely before breaking into pieces.

BOURBON BALLS

PREPARATION TIME: *30 minutes*
YIELD: *4 dozen*

1	**7½-ounce package vanilla wafers, finely crushed**
1	**cup chopped nuts**
2	**cups sifted powdered sugar**
2	**tablespoons cocoa**
1½	**tablespoons light corn syrup**
4	**ounces bourbon or rum**
	Powdered sugar

In large bowl, mix all ingredients together well. Chill dough until easy to handle, about 20 minutes. Roll into balls in palms of hands. Dust with powdered sugar.

These freeze beautifully and make a delightful gift.

CHOCOLATE SHERRY BARS

PREPARATION TIME: *1 hour, plus chilling time*
YIELD: *6-7 dozen*

BASE

4	ounces unsweetened chocolate
1	cup margarine
4	eggs
2	cups sugar
1	cup flour
½	teaspoon salt
1	teaspoon vanilla

FILLING

½	cup margarine
4	cups powdered sugar
¼	cup light cream
¼	cup sherry
1	cup chopped pecans

TOPPING

3	ounces semi-sweet chocolate chips (½ cup)
2	tablespoons margarine
1½	tablespoons water

In small saucepan, melt chocolate and margarine together over low heat. Cool. In large bowl, beat eggs until thick and lemon colored. Add sugar to eggs. Mix, then add chocolate mixture. Mix well. Mix flour and salt together. Add to sugar mixture. Add vanilla. Beat 1 minute. Pour into a greased and floured 10 x 14-inch jelly roll pan. Bake at 325 degrees for 25 minutes. Cool.

Beat together all filling ingredients. Spread over base and chill well.

In small saucepan, melt chocolate chips, margarine and water together over low heat and dribble over the filling. Refrigerate or freeze. Cut into 1-inch squares.

DOUBLE CHOCOLATE BROWNIES

PREPARATION TIME: *45 minutes plus freezing time*
YIELD: *16 2-inch squares*

6	ounces chocolate chips (1 cup)
¾	cup flour
¼	teaspoon baking soda
¼	teaspoon salt
5½	tablespoons butter
¾	cup sugar
2	tablespoons water
1	cup chocolate chips
1	teaspoon vanilla
2	eggs
¾	cup chopped pecans or walnuts
	Powdered sugar

Freeze 1 cup chocolate chips for 1 hour. In small bowl, combine flour, baking soda and salt. In saucepan, bring butter, sugar and water to a boil. Immediately remove from heat. Add 1 cup chocolate chips and vanilla, stirring until chips are melted and mixture is smooth. Transfer mixture to large bowl. Add eggs, one at a time, beating well after each addition. Gradually blend in flour mixture. Stir in nuts and frozen chocolate chips. Spread into a greased 9-inch square baking pan. Bake at 325 degrees for 30-35 minutes. Cool completely. Cut into squares. Sprinkle with powdered sugar.

PECAN-TOPPED TOFFEE

PREPARATION TIME: *1 hour, 20 minutes*
YIELD: *12-15 pieces*

1	cup butter (not margarine)
1	cup firmly packed brown sugar
6	1⅜-ounce milk chocolate bars
½	cup finely chopped pecans

In deep, narrow saucepan, combine butter and sugar. Cook over medium high heat, stirring constantly, until mixture reaches exactly 300 degrees on a candy thermometer (hard crack stage). Pour immediately into greased 9-inch square baking pan. Lay chocolate bars evenly over hot candy. When soft, spread into a smooth layer. Sprinkle nuts over chocolate and press in lightly with your fingers. Chill in refrigerator until chocolate is firm (no longer than 1 hour). Invert candy onto a flat surface and break apart into small, irregular pieces.

GRASSHOPPER BARS

PREPARATION TIME: *1 hour, 45 minutes*
YIELD: *20 bars*

BASE

1½	cups flour
2	cups sugar
¾	cup plus 2 tablespoons instant cocoa mix
1½	teaspoons salt
1	teaspoon baking powder
1⅓	cups butter, softened
4	eggs
2	teaspoons vanilla
2	tablespoons corn syrup
2	cups coarsely chopped nuts

In large bowl, mix together all base ingredients except nuts. Stir in nuts and pour into a greased 9 x 13-inch pan. Bake at 350 degrees until center is soft and edges are slightly firm, about 40-45 minutes. Do not overbake. Cool.

MINT FROSTING

2	cups powdered sugar
4	tablespoons butter, softened
2	tablespoons milk
	Green food coloring
½	teaspoon peppermint extract (or Crème de Menthe)

In small bowl, combine all frosting ingredients and spread over cooled base. Place in freezer for 15-20 minutes.

GLAZE

3	ounces unsweetened chocolate
3	tablespoons butter

In small saucepan or microwave, melt chocolate and butter together and pour evenly over frosting. Refrigerate until hard. Carefully cut into bars and remove from pan.

OLD-FASHIONED OATMEAL COOKIES

PREPARATION TIME: *45 minutes*
YIELD: *5 dozen*

1	cup butter, softened
1	teaspoon salt
2	teaspoons vanilla
2	tablespoons molasses
2	cups sugar
2	teaspoons cinnamon
2	eggs
2	cups flour
1½	teaspoons baking soda
2	cups quick oats
1½	cups raisins

In large bowl, combine butter, salt, vanilla, molasses, sugar, cinnamon and eggs. Beat thoroughly. Sift flour with soda. Add to butter mixture. Fold in oats and raisins. Drop on lightly greased baking sheet by teaspoons. Bake at 350 degrees for 10 minutes.

POPPY SEED COOKIES

PREPARATION TIME: *20 minutes plus chilling time*
YIELD: *5 dozen*

1	cup sugar
	Peel of one orange
1	egg yolk
1	cup unsalted butter, softened and cut into 8 pieces
½	teaspoon salt
½	teaspoon grated nutmeg
1	cup unbleached flour
1	cup cake flour
¼	cup poppy seeds

Combine sugar and orange peel in food processor and mince finely. Add yolk and process a few seconds. Add butter, salt and nutmeg and mix until light and fluffy, about 1 minute. Add remaining ingredients and mix using 4-5 on/off turns. Be careful not to overprocess. Divide dough into 4 equal portions and set each portion on a sheet of plastic wrap. Shape dough into 2 x 4-inch cylinders. Wrap tightly in plastic wrap and chill until firm, about 1 hour. Dough can be frozen at this point. Cut each cylinder into ¼-inch slices and set on baking sheets, 1½ inches apart. Bake at 350 degrees until edges are lightly browned, about 8 minutes. Transfer to wire rack and cool.

RASPBERRY BARS

PREPARATION TIME: *50 minutes*
YIELD: *20 large bars*

1 cup butter, softened
½ cup sugar
2 egg yolks, well beaten
2 cups flour
½ teaspoon baking powder
1 tablespoon lemon juice
1 teaspoon grated lemon peel
1 cup raspberry jam

In large bowl, cream butter and sugar. Add yolks. Sift flour and baking powder together and add alternately to butter mixture with lemon juice and peel. Divide dough in half. Line a jelly roll pan with half the dough and spread with jam. On a floured surface, roll other half of dough into a thin square. Cut into strips ½-inch wide. Arrange strips in lattice-fashion over the jam. Bake at 400 degrees until lightly browned, about 25 minutes. Cut into 2 x 3-inch bars while still slightly warm.

VANILLA BROWNIES

PREPARATION TIME: *45 minutes*
YIELD: *30 large brownies*

⅔ cup butter, melted
1 pound light brown sugar
3 eggs
2⅔ cups sifted flour
2½ teaspoons baking powder
½ teaspoon salt
1 12-ounce package semi-sweet chocolate chips (2 cups)
1 cup chopped pecans

In large bowl, add sugar to butter and blend well. Cool approximately 10 minutes. Beat in eggs, one at a time. Add flour, baking powder, salt, chocolate chips and pecans. Mix well. Spread in a greased 15½ x 10½-inch pan. Bake at 350 degrees for 25-30 minutes.

WHITE CHOCOLATE AND ALMOND COOKIES

PREPARATION TIME: *20 minutes*
YIELD: *4 dozen*

¾	**cup brown sugar, firmly packed**
½	**cup sugar**
½	**cup butter, softened**
½	**cup shortening**
1½	**teaspoons vanilla**
1	**egg**
1¾	**cups flour**
1	**teaspoon baking soda**
½	**teaspoon salt**
8	**ounces white chocolate, chopped**
¼	**cup sliced almonds**

In large bowl, combine brown sugar, sugar, butter, shortening, vanilla and egg. Blend well. Stir in flour, soda and salt. Blend well. Stir in white chocolate and almonds. Mix well. Drop by rounded teaspoonfuls, 2 inches apart, onto an ungreased baking sheet. Bake at 375 degrees until a light golden brown, about 8-10 minutes. Remove immediately.

APPLE WALNUT CRUMBLE

PREPARATION TIME: *1 hour, 45 minutes*
YIELD: *6 servings*

¾	cup oatmeal
1	cup brown sugar
2	teaspoons grated lemon rind
1	teaspoon baking powder
1	teaspoon cinnamon
½	teaspoon allspice
½	teaspoon nutmeg
¼	teaspoon salt
½	cup cold butter, cut into small pieces
2	cups finely chopped walnuts
2	pounds tart apples, peeled, cored, halved and thinly sliced crosswise
	Lightly whipped cream

In blender or food processor, grind oatmeal to a coarse powder and transfer to bowl. To oatmeal, add brown sugar, lemon rind, baking powder, cinnamon, allspice, nutmeg and salt. Combine well. Blend in butter until mixture resembles coarse meal. Stir in chopped nuts. Spread half of mixture in well greased, 1½-quart shallow oven-proof dish and press down lightly. Arrange apples over the mixture and sprinkle the remaining mixture over the apples. Bake at 375 degrees for 30 minutes. Let cool on a rack for 15 minutes. Serve with dollops of lightly whipped cream.

BASIC PIE CRUST

PREPARATION TIME: *45 minutes*
YIELD: *1 single crust*

1	**cup flour**
½	**teaspoon salt**
⅓	**cup shortening**
3-4	**tablespoons ice water**

In bowl, stir flour and salt together. Cut in shortening with a pastry blender or fork until the pieces are the size of small peas. Sprinkle 3 tablespoons ice water over the flour mixture and toss with a fork until all the flour is moistened and mixture starts to form a ball. If necessary, add remaining ice water to crumbs in bottom of bowl. Form into a ball, wrap in plastic wrap and refrigerate until ready to use. Roll out dough and place in a 9-inch pie pan.

For a baked crust, prick sides and bottom of dough with a fork. To lessen shrinkage, fit a piece of foil over the crust and fill with dried beans. Refrigerate for 15-20 minutes. Bake at 475 degrees for 8 minutes. Remove foil and beans and bake until the crust is golden brown, about 4-5 minutes.

This recipe can be doubled for a two-crust pie.

CHOCOLATE MINT PIE

PREPARATION TIME: *30 minutes plus chilling time*
YIELD: *6-8 servings*

5	egg yolks
¼	cup sugar
⅛	teaspoon salt
6	ounces semi-sweet chocolate chips, melted (1 cup)
3	tablespoons brandy
5	egg whites
¼	cup sugar
1	9-inch baked pie shell
1	cup heavy cream
2-3	tablespoons Crème de Menthe

In large bowl, combine egg yolks, ¼ cup sugar and salt. Beat at high speed until thick and lemon colored. Slowly blend in chocolate and then brandy. In separate bowl, beat egg whites until soft mounds form. Gradually add ¼ cup sugar. Continue beating until stiff. Fold in chocolate mixture. Gently place mixture in baked pie shell and chill for 2-4 hours. Whip heavy cream with Crème de Menthe until soft mounds form. Spread over top of pie and serve.

CHOCOLATE MOUSSE PIE

PREPARATION TIME: *1 hour, 30 minutes*
YIELD: *6-8 servings*

¼	cup graham cracker crumbs
8	ounces semi-sweet chocolate, coarsely chopped
1	teaspoon instant coffee dissolved in ¼ cup boiling water
8	egg yolks
⅔	cup sugar
1	teaspoon vanilla
8	egg whites
2	cups heavy cream
¼-½	cup powdered sugar

Grease a 9-inch pie pan and sprinkle with graham cracker crumbs. Pour excess out. Melt chocolate with dissolved coffee and water together in double boiler or microwave. Mix thoroughly. In bowl, beat egg yolks with sugar until fluffy. Add vanilla. Add chocolate mixture. Beat egg whites until very stiff. Fold into chocolate mixture. Divide the mixture in half. Put one half in the pie pan and bake at 375 degrees for 20 minutes. It will rise and fall to form a pie shell. Let cool. Chill the other half. When ready to serve, spread chilled portion on pie shell. Beat heavy cream with enough powdered sugar to sweeten, until peaks form. Spread on top of pie.

Sprinkle with shaved chocolate for an elegant effect.

CREAMY PUMPKIN PIE

PREPARATION TIME: *55 minutes*
YIELD: *6-8 servings*

FILLING

2	eggs
1	cup ricotta cheese
2	cups pumpkin, steamed, drained and mashed
¾	cup firmly packed light brown sugar
½	teaspoon salt
1½	teaspoons pumpkin pie spice
1	teaspoon vanilla
6	ounces evaporated milk
1	9-inch unbaked pie shell*
	Whipped cream
	Pecans or pumpkin seeds, toasted

See recipe for Basic Pie Crust on page 196.

In large bowl, beat eggs. Add cheese and beat until smooth. Stir in remaining filling ingredients and blend well.

Pour mixture into pie shell and bake at 375 degrees for 45 minutes. Cool on wire rack. Garnish with whipped cream and nuts.

FRESH FRUIT TART

PREPARATION TIME: *45 minutes plus chilling time*
YIELD: *10-12 servings*

CRUST
1	cup ground walnuts
8	tablespoons butter, softened
3	tablespoons sugar
1½	cups flour
1	egg yolk
½	teaspoon vanilla

In bowl, mix all crust ingredients together. Chill. Press into 13-inch tart pan. Bake at 350 degrees until crust begins to brown, about 20 minutes. Cool on wire rack.

CREAM CHEESE LAYER
1	8-ounce package cream cheese, softened
4	tablespoons sugar
1	egg
½	teaspoon vanilla
½	teaspoon lemon juice

Cream together all cream cheese layer ingredients. Spread over crust.

FRUIT
2	large peaches, sliced
2	kiwi, sliced
¼	cup blueberries

Arrange fruit in an attractive pattern on cream cheese layer.

GLAZE
1	package unflavored gelatin
2	tablespoons black raspberry liqueur
1	10-ounce jar red currant jelly

In small saucepan, combine gelatin and liqueur. Let soften 1 minute. Add jelly and stir over low heat until smooth. Remove from heat and cool slightly. Spoon half of glaze over fruit. Reserve remainder for another use. Refrigerate tart for 1 hour before serving.

Any fresh fruit can be used. Be creative with colors and design.

MOCHA ALASKAN PIE

PREPARATION TIME: *2 hours*
YIELD: *6-8 servings*

4	**tablespoons butter**
1	**cup chocolate wafer cookie crumbs, finely crushed**
1	**tablespoon sugar**
1	**quart coffee ice cream, slightly softened**
1	**5½-ounce can chocolate sauce**
½	**cup chopped pecans**
3	**egg whites**
½	**teaspoon vanilla**
¼	**teaspoon cream of tartar**
6	**tablespoons sugar**

Melt butter in saucepan and stir in cookie crumbs and 1 tablespoon sugar. Mix well. Press evenly over sides and bottom of 9-inch pie pan. Bake at 350 degrees for 10 minutes. Cool completely. Spread ice cream in cooled crust and freeze until firm. Drizzle chocolate sauce over ice cream and sprinkle with nuts. Freeze until firm. In small bowl, beat egg whites with vanilla and cream of tartar until soft peaks form. Add sugar, 1 tablespoon at a time, beating about 1 minute after each addition, until stiff peaks form. Swirl meringue evenly over pie, sealing to edge of crust. Freeze until firm. When frozen, wrap pie tightly in plastic wrap, being careful not to disturb meringue. To serve, place frozen pie, uncovered, in 450 degree oven until meringue is lightly browned, about 4 minutes.

An impressive dessert to have in the freezer for unexpected guests.

SOUR CREAM APPLE PIE

PREPARATION TIME: *1 hour, 10 minutes*
YIELD: *8 servings*

PIE

2	tablespoons flour
¾	cup sugar
1	egg
1	cup sour cream
1	teaspoon vanilla
½	teaspoon nutmeg
1¾	cups apples, peeled, cored and thinly sliced (about 2-3 apples)
1	9-inch unbaked pie shell*

TOPPING

⅓	cup sugar
⅓	cup flour
1	teaspoon cinnamon
4	tablespoons butter, softened

*See recipe for Basic Pie Crust on page 196.

Sift flour and sugar together. In large bowl, combine egg, sour cream, vanilla and nutmeg with flour mixture. Beat to thin batter. Stir in apples. Pour into pie shell. Bake at 400 degrees for 30 minutes.

In small bowl, mix all topping ingredients together until coarse crumbs form. Sprinkle over pie. Return pie to oven and bake for 10 minutes more.

APPLE CAKE

PREPARATION TIME: *2 hours, 30 minutes*
YIELD: *12-14 servings*

CAKE

2 cups sugar

3 eggs

1¼ cups cooking oil

¼ cup orange juice

3 cups flour

¼ teaspoon salt

1 teaspoon baking soda

½ teaspoon cinnamon

1 teaspoon vanilla

1¼ cups chopped apples (about 2 apples)

1 cup flaked coconut

1 cup chopped pecans

Combine all cake ingredients in order given. Bake in tube pan at 325 degrees for 1½ hours.

TOPPING

½ cup margarine

½ cup buttermilk

1 cup sugar

In small saucepan combine all topping ingredients. Bring to a boil. Spoon over cake as soon as it is removed from the oven. Let cool completely in pan. Invert onto cake plate.

Topping can be prepared in microwave oven by melting margarine first, then adding sugar and buttermilk. Cook on high power for three minutes, then stir.

BANANA NUT CAKE

PREPARATION TIME: *1 hour, 20 minutes*
YIELD: *10 servings*

CAKE
½ cup shortening

1½ cups sugar

2 eggs, beaten

2 cups cake flour

½ teaspoon baking soda

½ teaspoon salt

½ teaspoon baking powder

¼ cup sour milk*

1½ cups mashed bananas (about 3 bananas)

1 teaspoon vanilla

1 cup coarsely chopped walnuts

In large bowl, cream shortening and sugar together. Beat well. Add eggs and beat. Sift dry ingredients and add alternately with sour milk and bananas. Add vanilla and nuts. Bake at 350 degrees for 35-40 minutes in two ungreased 8-inch round cake pans. Frost when cool.

BUTTER FROSTING
5 tablespoons flour

1 cup milk

1 cup butter, softened

1 cup sugar

1 teaspoon vanilla

In medium saucepan, whisk together flour and milk. Boil, stirring constantly, until very thick. Cool. Cream butter, sugar and vanilla together. Add to the cooled flour mixture and beat for 20 minutes.

For sour milk, pour 1½ teaspoons vinegar into the bottom of a ¼-cup measure. Fill with milk and stir lightly. Let stand at room temperature until curdled, about 10 minutes.

BLACK FOREST TORTE

PREPARATION TIME: *45 minutes plus 1 hour*
YIELD: *12 servings*

CAKE
1¾ cups flour

1¾ cups sugar

1¼ teaspoons baking soda

1 teaspoon salt

¼ teaspoon baking powder

⅔ cup margarine, softened

4 ounces unsweetened chocolate, melted and cooled

1¼ cups water

1 teaspoon vanilla

3 eggs

CHOCOLATE FILLING
6 ounces German Sweet chocolate

1½ cups margarine

½ cup sliced almonds, toasted

WHIPPED CREAM FILLING
2 cups heavy cream

1 tablespoon powdered sugar

1 teaspoon vanilla

1 21-ounce can cherry pie filling

CHOCOLATE SCROLLS
1 1-ounce square semi-sweet chocolate

In large mixing bowl, combine all cake ingredients, except eggs, and mix at low speed. Beat at medium speed for 1 minute. Add eggs and beat 2 minutes longer. Divide batter evenly among 4 greased 9-inch round pans. Bake at 350 degrees for 15-18 minutes. Cool slightly and remove from pans. Cool thoroughly. Wrap each cake in plastic wrap and freeze until ready to assemble.

Melt chocolate, then stir in margarine. Let cool. Stir in nuts.

Beat cream with sugar and vanilla until stiff. Do not overbeat.

Assemble torte 1-2 hours before serving. Place one frozen layer of cake on serving plate. Spread with half of chocolate filling. Let chocolate harden slightly, then spread with half of cherry pie filling. Top with another frozen cake layer. Spread with half of whipped cream filling. Top with third frozen cake layer. Spread with remaining chocolate filling. Top with remaining cherry filling. Place last cake layer on top. Spread with remaining whipped cream filling.

To make chocolate scrolls, allow square of semi-sweet chocolate to warm slightly. Using a vegetable peeler, peel scrolls from chocolate onto a plate. Refrigerate until firm. Garnish cake with scrolls.

CITRUS CHEESECAKE

PREPARATION TIME: *2 hours plus chilling time*
YIELD: *16 servings*

CRUST

- 1 **cup sifted flour**
- ¼ **cup sugar**
- 1 **teaspoon grated lemon peel**
- ½ **teaspoon vanilla**
- 1 **egg yolk**
- 4 **tablespoons butter, softened**

In medium bowl, combine flour, sugar, lemon peel and vanilla. Make a well in center and add egg yolk and butter. Mix with fingertips until dough cleans side of bowl. Form into a ball. Wrap in wax paper and refrigerate about 1 hour. Grease bottom and side of a 9-inch springform pan. Remove side from pan. Roll ⅓ of dough on bottom of the pan. Trim edge. Bake at 400 degrees until golden, about 8-10 minutes. Meanwhile, divide rest of dough into 3 parts. Roll each part into a 2½ x 10-inch strip. Put together springform pan with baked crust on bottom. Fit strips to side of pan, joining ends of strips, lining inside completely. Trim dough so it comes only ¾ up side. Chill until ready to fill.

FILLING

- 5 **8-ounce packages cream cheese, softened**
- 1¾ **cups sugar**
- 3 **tablespoons flour**
- 1½ **teaspoons grated lemon peel**
- 1½ **teaspoons grated orange peel**
- ¼ **teaspoon vanilla**
- 5 **eggs**
- 2 **egg yolks**
- ¼ **cup heavy cream**

In large bowl of electric mixer, combine cream cheese, sugar, flour, lemon peel, orange peel and vanilla. Beat at high speed until just blended. Beat in eggs and yolks, one at a time. Add heavy cream, beating just until well combined. Pour into crust in springform pan. Bake at 500 degrees for 10 minutes. Reduce heat to 250 degrees and bake 1 hour, 20 minutes more. Cool completely. Refrigerate until ready to serve.

Top with Pineapple Glaze or Strawberry Glaze on page 206.

PINEAPPLE GLAZE

PREPARATION TIME: *40 minutes*
YIELD: *covers one cheesecake*

2 **tablespoons sugar**	
4 **teaspoons cornstarch**	
2 **8¼-ounce cans crushed pineapple in heavy syrup, with liquid**	
2 **tablespoons lemon juice**	

In saucepan, combine sugar and cornstarch. Mix well. Stir in crushed pineapple, with liquid. Bring to a boil, stirring over medium heat. Boil 1 minute. Mixture will be thickened and translucent. Remove from heat and let cool slightly. Add lemon juice. Let cool completely. Spoon glaze over top of cheesecake.

STRAWBERRY GLAZE

PREPARATION TIME: *40 minutes*
YIELD: *covers one cheesecake*

2 **1-pound packages frozen whole strawberries, thawed**	
2 **tablespoons sugar**	
1 **tablespoon cornstarch**	
2 **teaspoons lemon juice**	

Drain strawberries well, reserving ¾ cup liquid. In saucepan, combine sugar and cornstarch. Mix well. Stir in reserved liquid. Bring to a boil, stirring over medium heat. Boil 1 minute. Mixture will be thickened and translucent. Remove from heat. Let cool slightly. Add lemon juice. Let cool completely. Arrange strawberries, with points up, over cooled cheesecake. Spoon glaze over strawberries.

CHOCOLATE GÂTEAU

PREPARATION TIME: *1 hour, 30 minutes*
YIELD: *12 servings*

GÂTEAU

5	ounces semi-sweet chocolate
⅔	cup butter, softened
¾	cup sugar
3	egg yolks
⅔	cup flour
¼	cup milk
½	cup finely ground blanched almonds
½	teaspoon vanilla
3	egg whites
½	teaspoon salt

Melt chocolate in double boiler. Set aside. In large bowl, cream butter at medium speed until smooth. Beat in sugar, 2 tablespoons at a time, and continue beating until light and fluffy. Beat in egg yolks, and continue beating until very light. Add melted chocolate and beat well. At low speed, beat in flour and milk alternately, beginning and ending with flour. Stir in ½ cup almonds and vanilla. Beat egg whites with salt at high speed until stiff peaks form. Gently fold whites into batter until just combined. Turn into lightly greased 9-inch springform pan and spread evenly. Bake at 350 degrees until cake tester inserted in center comes out clean, about 25-30 minutes. Cool 10 minutes in pan on wire rack. With spatula, loosen edges and remove sides.

ICING

5	ounces semi-sweet chocolate
3	tablespoons milk
4	tablespoons butter
1	cup powdered sugar
¼	teaspoon almond extract
½	cup finely ground blanched almonds
	Sliced almonds

In double boiler, melt chocolate with milk and butter. Remove from heat. Add powdered sugar and almond extract, beating until smooth. Frost top and sides of cake. Sprinkle remaining ½ cup almonds on top and decorate edges with sliced almonds, overlapping them.

Use top quality chocolate for this elegant cake.

FUDGE CAKE

PREPARATION TIME: *3 hours*
YIELD: *8 servings*

2	cups flour
1	teaspoon baking soda
⅛	teaspoon salt
1¾	cups coffee
¼	cup bourbon
5	ounces unsweetened chocolate, chopped
1	cup butter, cut into pieces
2	cups sugar
2	eggs
1	teaspoon vanilla
1	cup heavy cream
1	tablespoon sugar
2-3	tablespoons white crème de cacao

Sift flour, soda and salt together. In double boiler, heat coffee and bourbon together for 5 minutes. Add chocolate and butter, stirring until both are melted and mixture is smooth. Remove from heat and stir in sugar. Let mixture cool for 3 minutes and transfer to bowl of electric mixer. Gradually add flour mixture to chocolate mixture and continue to beat at medium speed for 1 minute. Add eggs and vanilla and beat until batter is smooth. Pour into a greased 9-inch tube pan that has been dusted with cocoa. Bake at 275 degrees until cake tester inserted in the center comes out clean, about 1½ hours. Cool cake completely in pan on wire rack. In chilled bowl, beat heavy cream with sugar and crème de cacao until soft peaks form. Turn cake out of pan on serving plate. Serve with sweetened whipped cream.

SOUR CREAM CAKE

PREPARATION TIME: *2 hours*
YIELD: *20 servings*

1	cup butter, softened
3	cups sugar
6	egg yolks
3	cups flour
¼	teaspoon baking soda
1	cup sour cream
2	tablespoons almond extract
1	teaspoon vanilla
6	egg whites

In large bowl, cream butter and sugar together. Add egg yolks, one at a time, beating well after each addition. Sift flour three times. Mix baking soda into sour cream. To butter mixture, add flour and sour cream alternately. Add almond extract and vanilla. Beat egg whites until stiff peaks form. Fold into batter. Pour into a greased and floured tube pan and bake at 300 degrees for 1½ hours.

For a festive dessert, serve with strawberries and whipped cream.

ITALIAN CREAM CAKE

PREPARATION TIME: *1 hour, 30 minutes*
YIELD: *16 servings*

CAKE
½	**cup butter, softened**
½	**cup cooking oil**
2	**cups sugar**
5	**egg yolks**
1	**teaspoon baking soda**
1	**cup buttermilk**
2	**cups flour**
1	**teaspoon vanilla**
1	**cup chopped pecans**
1	**cup coconut (optional)**
5	**egg whites**

In large bowl, cream together butter and oil. Gradually add sugar. Add egg yolks, one at a time, mixing well after each addition. Stir baking soda into buttermilk. Alternately add buttermilk and flour to mixture. Add vanilla, pecans and coconut. Beat egg whites until very stiff and fold into batter. Divide batter evenly among 3 greased 9-inch cake pans and bake at 325 degrees for 30 minutes. Let cool for 15 minutes and remove from pans.

ICING
1	**16-ounce box powdered sugar**
½	**cup butter, softened**
1	**8-ounce package cream cheese, softened**
1	**teaspoon vanilla**

Combine all icing ingredients and mix well. Frost layers, sides and top of cake.

For variation, frost cake as a torte, just frosting between layers and on top.

CHOCOLATE-VANILLA CHARLOTTE

PREPARATION TIME: *3 hours*
YIELD: *4-6 servings*

1⅓ cups Vanilla Sauce*

1½ teaspoons unflavored gelatin

1½ tablespoons cold water

24 Ladyfingers*

2 cups Chocolate Mousse*

3 cups Sweetened Whipped Cream*

Chocolate, shaved or grated

Sprinkle gelatin over cold water to soften for 5 minutes. Stir softened gelatin into Vanilla Sauce while the sauce is still warm. Cool sauce by placing the cooking pan into ice water. Stir frequently until sauce is cold and very thick. Set aside. Grease sides of a straight-sided charlotte mold (6¼-inch wide) and place Ladyfingers against sides of mold. If necessary, cut Ladyfingers off at rim of mold. Fill mold halfway with Chocolate Mousse. Chill 30 minutes. Reserve ¾ cup Sweetened Whipped Cream for later use. Fold remaining cream into cold Vanilla Sauce. Pour this mixture on top of Chocolate Mousse and fill mold completely. Chill at least 1 hour. To serve, dip mold into hot water for a few seconds and turn upside down on a platter. Decorate top with reserved Sweetened Whipped Cream and shaved chocolate.

Recipe follows.

Well worth the effort!

VANILLA SAUCE

PREPARATION TIME: *20 minutes*
YIELD: *1⅓ cups*

1	cup milk
½	vanilla bean, split lengthwise
3	egg yolks
⅓	cup sugar

In saucepan, bring milk and vanilla bean to a boil. Reduce heat to low, cover and let vanilla bean infuse for 10 minutes. Beat yolks and sugar on medium speed until mixture is light colored and forms a ribbon. Beating constantly, add milk to yolks. Pour mixture back into saucepan and heat slowly, stirring constantly. Do not boil. When liquid coats spoon, remove pan from heat and place immediately in bowl of cold water to stop cooking. Remove vanilla bean. If sauce should separate, blend at high speed or vigorously shake small amounts at a time in a jar.

CHOCOLATE MOUSSE

PREPARATION TIME: *30 minutes*
YIELD: *2 cups*

4½	ounces semi-sweet chocolate
5½	tablespoons butter, cut in pieces
2	egg yolks
3	egg whites (½ cup)
1½	tablespoons sugar

In double boiler, melt chocolate. Remove from heat and add butter, stirring until completely melted. Let mixture cool completely until it is the consistency of very thick cream. Stir in yolks, one at a time. Beat egg whites until soft peaks form. Add sugar and continue beating until stiff peaks form. Fold chocolate mixture into whites, making sure they are perfectly blended together.

SWEETENED WHIPPED CREAM

PREPARATION TIME: *5 minutes*
YIELD: *3 cups*

1½	**cups heavy cream**
1½	**teaspoons sugar**
½	**teaspoon vanilla**

In a chilled bowl, beat heavy cream with sugar and vanilla until peaks form.

LADYFINGERS

PREPARATION TIME: *30 minutes*
YIELD: *24 ladyfingers*

5	**egg yolks**
⅔	**cup sugar, less 1½ tablespoons**
1	**cup flour**
1½	**tablespoons sugar**
5	**egg whites**
	Powdered sugar

In large bowl, beat yolks at medium speed and gradually beat in ⅔ cup less 1½ tablespoons sugar. Continue beating until mixture is thick, pale and forms a ribbon, about 3 minutes. Carefully stir in flour, working the mixture as little as possible. Beat egg whites for 1½ minutes at high speed. Add 1½ tablespoons sugar and continue beating 1½ minutes more. Fold egg whites into yolk batter quickly and carefully. Line 2 baking sheets with parchment paper, placing a little batter under each corner of the paper to make it stick to the baking sheets. Fit a pastry bag with a ¾-inch (2 cm.) round metal nozzle and fill with batter. Squeeze out 24 ladyfingers, 3½ inches long, onto baking sheets. Dust with powdered sugar and bake for 18 minutes. Check after first 12 minutes to see if baking sheets need to be turned for even browning.

Greased and floured baking sheets work well if you do not have parchment paper.
Two teaspoons orange-flower water or the grated peel of ½ lemon can be added to the batter if ladyfingers are going to be eaten plain. Store in airtight container.

GRAND MARNIER CHOCOLATE MOUSSE TORTE

PREPARATION TIME: *50 minutes plus freezing time*
YIELD: *12 servings*

CRUST

1½ cups chocolate wafer cookies, crushed

½ cup unsalted butter, melted

FILLING

1 pound semi-sweet chocolate, coarsely chopped

2 eggs

2 egg yolks

¼ cup Grand Marnier

2 cups heavy cream

4 egg whites

¼ teaspoon salt

TOPPING

1 cup heavy cream

1 tablespoon Grand Marnier

Chocolate Scrolls*

Combine crumbs and butter in food processor. Press onto bottom and sides of an ungreased 8 x 3-inch springform pan. The mixture should come close to top of pan. Refrigerate crust.

Melt chocolate in double boiler, stirring occasionally. When melted completely, remove from double boiler. Cool to lukewarm. Add 2 eggs and 2 egg yolks to chocolate. Whisk briskly, blending well. Add ¼ cup Grand Marnier and continue stirring until mixture is smooth and creamy. Whip 2 cups cream until almost stiff. Beat egg whites with salt until stiff, but not dry. Stir a little of both whipped cream and egg whites into chocolate mixture. Alternately fold in remaining whites and whipped cream in two or three additions each. Turn into prepared crust and shake gently to level. Freeze torte until filling is firm enough so that topping can be spread over it.

Whip 1 cup cream until soft peaks form. Gradually beat in 1 tablespoon Grand Marnier and continue beating until fairly stiff. Spread smoothly over chilled filling. Return torte to freezer and freeze for at least 24 hours. To serve, run sharp knife around the edges of pan to release crust. Remove springform sides. Garnish with Chocolate Scrolls.

See recipe for Chocolate Scrolls on page 204.

LEMON SOUFFLÉ

PREPARATION TIME: *2 hours*
YIELD: *6 servings*

1 package unflavored gelatin	In small saucepan, soften gelatin in water. Add peel, lemon juice and sugar. Stir over low heat until gelatin is thoroughly dissolved. Chill to a syrupy consistency. Beat egg whites until very stiff. Fold into lemon mixture. Whip cream until stiff and fold into lemon mixture. Mix thoroughly. Place a wax paper collar around a 1-quart soufflé dish. Pour lemon mixture into dish and refrigerate until set.
2 tablespoons water	
Grated peel of 4 lemons	
½ cup strained fresh lemon juice	
1 cup super-fine sugar	
1 cup egg whites (about 6 egg whites)	
1 cup heavy cream	

Garnish with lemon slices and fresh mint, and serve with additional whipped cream.

LITTLE POTS OF CHOCOLATE

PREPARATION TIME: *5 minutes plus chilling time*
YIELD: *4 servings*

¾ cup heavy cream	Heat cream. In food processor, with machine running, combine chocolate, eggs, coffee and rum. Scrape down sides of work bowl. Again with machine running, pour hot cream through tube and process until chocolate is melted. Pour into ramekins, demitasse cups or chocolate pots. Refrigerate until set or freeze for 1 hour.
6 ounces semi-sweet chocolate, grated	
2 eggs	
2 tablespoons strong black coffee	
2 tablespoons dark rum	

Little Pots of Chocolate are a great emergency dessert. They can be prepared in less than 5 minutes with ingredients usually available in most kitchens.
The success of this recipe depends on the use of top quality chocolate.

ORANGE STEAMED PUDDING WITH ORANGE HARD SAUCE

PREPARATION TIME: *2 hours, 45 minutes*
YIELD: *8 servings*

PUDDING

½ cup unsalted butter, softened
1 cup sugar
4 eggs
2 cups flour
2 teaspoons baking powder
½ cup orange juice
1½ tablespoons grated orange peel
1½ tablespoons grated lemon peel

In large bowl, cream butter. Add sugar, a little at a time, and continue beating until mixture is light and fluffy. Add eggs, one at a time, beating well after each addition. Sift flour and baking powder together and add to butter mixture alternately with orange juice. Stir in orange peel and lemon peel. Pour batter into well-greased 1-quart steamed pudding mold and cover tightly with lid. Place mold on rack in kettle with tight fitting lid. Add enough hot water to kettle to reach two-thirds up sides of mold. Steam pudding, covered, for 2 hours over moderate heat. Remove mold from kettle and let stand on rack, uncovered, for 15 minutes. Invert pudding onto a plate. Dust with powdered sugar.

ORANGE HARD SAUCE

6 tablespoons unsalted butter, softened
1 cup sifted powdered sugar
1 tablespoon grated orange peel
2 teaspoons orange juice
Powdered sugar

Cream butter. Beat in powdered sugar, a little at a time. Add orange peel and orange juice and beat mixture until fluffy. Transfer to a serving bowl.

In place of a pudding mold, use a 1-quart charlotte mold or soufflé dish, covered tightly with a double layer of foil secured with kitchen string.

WHITE CHOCOLATE MOUSSE

PREPARATION TIME: *30 minutes plus chilling time*
YIELD: *8-10 servings*

1	envelope unflavored gelatin
3	tablespoons cold water
½	cup plus 1 tablespoon sugar
3	egg yolks
2	eggs
2	tablespoons cornstarch
2	cups milk
6	ounces white chocolate, melted
3	egg whites
3	tablespoons sugar
2	tablespoons white crème de cacao
2	cups heavy cream
	Chocolate Scrolls*

Soften gelatin in cold water. Set aside. In another bowl, combine ½ cup plus 1 tablespoon sugar with egg yolks and 2 eggs. Mix cornstarch with small amount of milk to form paste and blend into egg mixture. Bring remaining milk to a boil and gradually stir into egg mixture. Cook entire mixture, stirring until thickened. Add gelatin mixture and melted chocolate. Set aside to cool. Beat egg whites with 3 tablespoons sugar and liqueur. Fold into custard. Whip cream and fold into custard mixture. Chill. Garnish with Chocolate Scrolls.

*See recipe for Chocolate Scrolls on page 204.

CHOCK FULL OF CHOCOLATE ICE CREAM

PREPARATION TIME: *1 hour plus freezing time*
YIELD: *1½-2 quarts*

3	ounces unsweetened chocolate, coarsely chopped
1	14-ounce can sweetened condensed milk
1½	teaspoons vanilla
4	tablespoons unsalted butter
3	egg yolks
2	ounces semi-sweet chocolate
½	cup strong black coffee
¾	cup sugar
½	cup light cream
1½	teaspoons dark rum
2	tablespoons white crème de cacao
2	cups heavy cream
2	ounces unsweetened chocolate, finely grated
¼	teaspoon salt

In double boiler, melt 3 ounces unsweetened chocolate. Add milk, stirring until smooth. Stir in vanilla and remove from heat. Cut butter into four equal pieces and add, one piece at a time, constantly stirring until all butter has been incorporated. Beat yolks until light and lemon colored. Gradually stir in chocolate mixture and continue stirring until smooth and creamy. Set aside. In double boiler, heat 2 ounces semi-sweet chocolate, coffee, sugar and light cream. Stir constantly until smooth. Stir in rum and crème de cacao and allow mixture to cool to room temperature. Combine both chocolate mixtures, heavy cream, grated unsweetened chocolate and salt in large bowl. Pour mixture into canister of ice cream freezer and freeze according to manufacturer's directions.

Very, very rich.

CREAMY MAPLE ICE CREAM

PREPARATION TIME: *1 hour plus freezing time*
YIELD: *12 servings*

¾	cup sugar
¼	cup water
3-4	tablespoons milk
2	cups light cream
3-4	tablespoons milk
3	tablespoons flour
3	eggs
1¼	cups sugar
3	cups heavy cream
2	cups light cream
2	teaspoons vanilla
1	teaspoon maple flavoring
2	cups chopped walnuts or pecans

Caramelize sugar by heating ¾ cup sugar with water over high heat until sugar is melted and mixture is a rich caramel color. Be sure to wash down sugar crystals on sides of pan with pastry brush dipped in water while mixture is boiling. Remove from heat and immediately stir in milk until caramelized sugar is liquified. Heat 2 cups light cream and add to caramelized mixture. Set aside. Add enough milk to flour to make a thin paste. Set aside. Beat eggs. Gradually add 1¼ cups sugar to eggs, beating constantly. Beat in flour paste. Add this mixture to caramelized mixture and cook until mixture is the consistency of thin gravy. Let cool (may refrigerate to facilitate cooling). When cool, add heavy cream, 2 cups light cream, vanilla, maple flavoring and nuts. Stir to mix. Freeze in canister of ice cream freezer according to manufacturer's instructions.

Serve with your favorite chocolate cake or brownies. Very rich.

LEMON ICE CREAM

PREPARATION TIME: *10 minutes plus freezing time*
YIELD: *4-6 servings*

¼	cup lemon juice
1	tablespoon grated lemon peel
1	cup sugar
2	cups light cream
	Yellow food coloring

Mix all ingredients together and freeze in an ice cream freezer according to manufacturer's instructions.

A delicious, light dessert.

PEPPERMINT ICE CREAM

PREPARATION TIME: *5 minutes plus freezing time*
YIELD: *1½ quarts*

2 **8-inch peppermint candy canes (or 32 hard peppermint candies)**	Crush candy. Pour heavy cream and light cream into ice cream canister. Add sugar, vanilla and salt. Stir until sugar is dissolved. Add candy and stir. Freeze according to manufacturer's instructions. Transfer to another container and place in refrigerator freezer for 1-2 hours before serving.
2 **cups heavy cream**	
2 **cups light cream**	
½ **cup sugar**	
1½ **teaspoons vanilla**	
⅛ **teaspoon salt**	

Serve with Old Fashioned Hot Fudge Sauce on page 221.

APPLE-FILLED CRÊPES AND HONEY BUTTER

PREPARATION TIME: *1 hour, 5 minutes*
YIELD: *6-8 servings*

CRÊPES

4 **eggs**	To make crêpe batter, blend eggs, sour cream, flour, honey and milk until smooth. Let stand for 1 hour. Make crepes using melted butter to grease pan.
¾ **cup sour cream**	
¾ **cup sifted flour**	
¼ **cup honey**	
¼ **cup milk**	
Melted butter	

FILLING

4 **cups peeled, cored and sliced apples (about 5 apples)**	In bowl, combine apples, sugar and ½ teaspoon cinnamon. Divide mixture among crêpes, roll up and arrange, seam side down, in one layer in greased baking dish.
⅓ **cup sugar**	
½ **teaspoon cinnamon**	

HONEY BUTTER

1¼ **cups unsalted butter, softened**	In small bowl, cream together butter and honey until mixture is smooth. Spoon 1 tablespoon honey butter over each crepe and sprinkle with remaining ½ teaspoon cinnamon. Bake at 375 degrees for 20 minutes. Serve with remaining honey butter.
½ **cup honey**	
½ **teaspoon cinnamon**	

CHOCOLATE-DIPPED STRAWBERRIES WITH ORANGE CREAM

PREPARATION TIME: *1 hour*
YIELD: *4-6 servings*

24	**large strawberries, stems attached**
	Orange-flavored liqueur
8	**ounces semi-sweet chocolate, chopped**
¾	**cup heavy cream**
1	**tablespoon powdered sugar**
1	**tablespoon orange-flavored liqueur**

Inject strawberries with orange-flavored liqueur and let stand at room temperature, for 30 minutes. Melt chocolate in double boiler, stirring constantly, until mixture reaches 125 degrees on candy thermometer. Remove from heat and let chocolate cool to 85 degrees. Maintain chocolate at 85 degrees by periodically setting pan over warm water. Holding stem, dip each strawberry in chocolate, letting excess chocolate drip back into pan. Place berries on baking sheet lined with greased wax paper. Allow chocolate to harden. Beat heavy cream until soft peaks form. Beat in powdered sugar and continue beating until stiff peaks form. Fold in 1 tablespoon orange-flavored liqueur. Serve strawberries on individual dessert plates with a dollop of orange cream alongside.

High quality chocolate is essential for best results and taste.
For buffet or cocktail party serve Orange Cream in a separate bowl for dipping.

CASHEW CARAMEL SAUCE

PREPARATION TIME: *10 minutes*
YIELD: *1½ cups*

¾ cup heavy cream

⅔ cup firmly packed brown sugar

3 egg yolks, slightly beaten

¼ teaspoon salt

3 tablespoons butter

1 tablespoon lemon juice

1 teaspoon vanilla

⅔ cup coarsely chopped salted cashews

Place heavy cream, sugar, egg yolks and salt in small, heavy saucepan. Cook over low heat, stirring frequently, until thick and creamy. Add butter, 1 tablespoon at a time, stirring constantly. Remove from heat. Stir in lemon juice and vanilla. Cool slightly. Just before serving, stir in cashews. Serve over ice cream.

OLD-FASHIONED HOT FUDGE SAUCE

PREPARATION TIME: *5 minutes*
YIELD: *⅔ cup*

2 1-ounce squares unsweetened chocolate

½ cup corn syrup

Salt to taste

½ teaspoon vanilla

1 teaspoon butter

Melt chocolate in top of double boiler over hot, but not boiling, water. Stir in corn syrup. Remove from heat. Add salt, vanilla and butter. Serve warm.

Exceptionally easy and delicious hot fudge sauce.

SOUTHWESTERN PLEASURES

Olé

GUACAMOLE

PREPARATION TIME: *15 minutes*
YIELD: *2 cups*

2	large avocados
1	large tomato, peeled, finely chopped and drained
1	large onion, finely chopped
2	tablespoons lemon juice
1	clove garlic, minced
½	teaspoon salt
1	teaspoon minced jalapeño chili, (optional)

Peel, pit and mash avocados. Reserve 1 pit. Mix all ingredients together. Blend well. Place avocado pit in guacamole to prevent discoloration. Remove at serving time.

Serve with corn chips or as an accompaniment to enchiladas or other Mexican dishes.

SALADA DE JICAMA

PREPARATION TIME: *10 minutes plus soaking time*
YIELD: *8 servings*

1	Bermuda onion, thinly sliced
2	tablespoons fresh lemon juice
2	tablespoons fresh lime juice
½	teaspoon grated lemon peel
¼	teaspoon salt
¾	cup olive oil
6	tablespoons peanut oil
1	head red leaf lettuce
1¾	pounds jicama, peeled and cut into matchstick juliennes

Cover onion with lightly salted water and soak for 2 hours. For vinaigrette, blend juices, lemon peel and salt in small bowl. Whisk in both oils in slow stream. Drain onion and pat dry. Transfer to large bowl. Add jicama. Toss with vinaigrette. Arrange lettuce leaves on platter or individual plates. Mound jicama and onion mixture onto lettuce.

This colorful, crunchy salad is just the right addition to a southwestern meal.

FIESTA SALSA

PREPARATION TIME: *15 minutes*
YIELD: *2 cups*

4	fresh tomatoes, chopped
2	fresh green chilies, finely chopped (or 1 4-ounce can chopped green chilies)
1	large Bermuda onion, chopped
1	green bell pepper, chopped
1	tablespoon sugar
1	tablespoon red wine vinegar
1	teaspoon olive oil
	Salt and pepper to taste
2	tablespoons chopped fresh cilantro
¼	teaspoon oregano

Mix all ingredients and refrigerate.

A mild salsa that can be used on tacos and enchiladas. Especially good heated and poured over thinly sliced strips of steak or roast beef. For spicier taste, use more green chilies.

MEXICAN STUFFED CHEESE

PREPARATION TIME: *1 hour*
YIELD: *8 servings*

1 2-pound round longhorn cheese

1 15-ounce can refried beans

1 4-ounce can diced green chilies, drained

1 medium tomato, seeded and chopped

2 cloves garlic, minced

¼ teaspoon oregano

¼ teaspoon coriander

¼ teaspoon Tabasco sauce

Oil

5 corn tortillas

Tortilla chips

Using a grapefruit knife and spoon, hollow out cheese, leaving a shell about ½-inch thick. Reserve scooped out cheese. In medium saucepan, combine beans, green chilies, tomato, garlic, oregano, coriander and Tabasco sauce. Cook until mixture is heated through. Set aside. Pour oil ½-inch deep in large skillet. Cook each tortilla, one at a time, for a few seconds only. Drain and pat dry. Line a quiche or similar type pan with overlapping tortillas. Place cheese shell in center and fill with bean mixture. Cover with reserved cheese. Bake at 375 degrees for 45 minutes. Serve with tortilla chips.

TORTILLA DE QUESO (TORTILLA ROLL-UPS)

PREPARATION TIME: *10 minutes*
YIELD: *1 dozen*

1 4-ounce can chopped green chilies

1 bunch scallions, chopped

1 clove garlic, minced

Salt to taste

2 8-ounce packages cream cheese, softened

12 large flour tortillas

Mix together green chilies, scallions, garlic and salt to taste. Blend into cream cheese. Spread thin layer of cream cheese mixture on each tortilla. Roll up and slice into bite-size pieces. Serve with Fiesta Salsa.

May be frozen whole and then sliced before serving.

SALADA DE PEPINO RECHEADO (STUFFED CUCUMBER SALAD)

PREPARATION TIME: *30 minutes plus overnight*
YIELD: *6-8 servings*

4	**8-inch cucumbers**
½	**teaspoon salt**
4	**3-ounce packages cream cheese**
2	**tablespoons grated onion**
3	**tablespoons finely chopped green bell pepper**
3	**tablespoons finely chopped red bell pepper**
1	**teaspoon paprika**
	Salt and pepper to taste
4-6	**large lettuce leaves**
2	**tomatoes, peeled, seeded and quartered**
	Mayonnaise

Cut off the ends of the cucumbers and score the skin lengthwise. Halve crosswise and remove the seedy centers of each half with an apple corer. Sprinkle the hollowed-out surfaces with salt and place on a rack to drain. Combine cream cheese, onion, peppers and paprika. Salt and pepper to taste. Stuff cucumbers with mixture. Wrap each cucumber half in aluminum foil and refrigerate overnight. When ready to serve, slice crosswise and arrange on a bed of lettuce. Garnish with tomatoes and serve with mayonnaise.

MEXICAN FRUIT PUNCH

PREPARATION TIME: *5 minutes*
YIELD: *6-8 servings*

1	**12-ounce can frozen pineapple juice concentrate**
1½	**cups water**
1	**cup freshly squeezed orange juice**
1	**cup freshly squeezed lemon juice**
1	**cup tequila (optional)**
⅔	**cup triple sec (optional)**
1	**cup mineral water or club soda**
5	**scoops pineapple sherbet**

In a glass bowl that will hold at least 2 quarts, combine pineapple juice concentrate with 1½ cups water. Add fruit juices. Add tequila and triple sec if desired. Just before serving, stir in mineral water and float sherbet. Stir several times.

CHOCOLATE MEXICANO

PREPARATION TIME: *15 minutes*
YIELD: *4 servings*

1 3-ounce tablet Mexican spiced chocolate (or 3 ounces semi-sweet chocolate, 2 tablespoons sugar, ½ teaspoon cinnamon, and ¼ teaspoon vanilla)

3 cups milk

Place chocolate tablet (or substitute) and milk in a saucepan. Bring to a boil. When chocolate has softened, beat mixture with a molinillo or a rotary beater until blended and mixture stops boiling. Bring to a boil again and beat well. Bring to a boil a third time and beat to produce as much foam as possible. Pour into cups and serve immediately.

GAZPACHO

PREPARATION TIME: *30 minutes plus chilling time*
YIELD: *6 servings*

3 pounds tomatoes, peeled, seeded and chopped

2 cucumbers, peeled, seeded and chopped

½ cup minced green bell pepper

½ cup minced onion

2 cups tomato juice

⅓ cup olive oil

3 tablespoons vinegar

1 clove garlic, minced

Juice of 1 lemon

¼ teaspoon Tabasco sauce

½ teaspoon paprika

Salt and pepper to taste

6 cubes of frozen tomato juice

In large bowl, combine tomatoes, cucumbers, green bell pepper, onion and tomato juice. In small bowl, mix oil, vinegar, garlic, lemon juice, Tabasco sauce and paprika. Add to tomato mixture. Salt and pepper to taste. Cover and chill soup for 4 hours or more. Serve in chilled bowls with a tomato juice ice cube.

Garnish with croutons or a dollop of sour cream.

SOPA DE LIMA (LIME AND TORTILLA SOUP)

PREPARATION TIME: *45 minutes*
YIELD: *6 servings*

1	**large red bell pepper, seeded and chopped**
1	**onion, minced**
1	**clove garlic, minced**
2	**tablespoons oil**
2	**tomatoes, peeled, seeded and chopped**
3	**fresh jalapeño or serrano chilies, seeded and minced (wear rubber gloves)**
6	**cups chicken broth**
1	**lime, halved crosswise and juiced (reserve the juice and shells)**
3	**tablespoons oil**
6	**small corn tortillas, halved and cut crosswise into ½-inch strips**
1½	**cups cooked and shredded chicken breast**
	Salt and pepper to taste.
6	**lime slices**

In saucepan, cook green bell pepper, onion and garlic in 2 tablespoons of oil over low heat, stirring until pepper is softened. Add tomatoes and cook, stirring, for 2 minutes. Add chilies, broth, lime juice and shells. Bring the liquid to a boil and simmer for 5 minutes. Discard lime shells. In large skillet, heat remaining 3 tablespoons of oil over moderate heat until hot, but not smoking. Cook tortilla strips in batches, stirring until golden and crisp, about 30 seconds to 1 minute. Transfer strips to paper towels to drain. Keep strips warm in a 250 degree oven. Add chicken to broth mixture and simmer until chicken is heated through. Season soup with salt and pepper. To serve, ladle into bowls. Add some fried tortilla strips. Float a lime slice in the center of each serving.

For a milder soup, substitute 2 mild, long green chilies, roasted, peeled and chopped, or 1 4-ounce can chopped green chilies.

SHRIMP AND GREEN CHILIES

PREPARATION TIME: *1 hour*
YIELD: *6-8 servings*

¾	**cup rice**
4	**tablespoons butter**
4	**celery stalks, chopped**
1	**green bell pepper, chopped**
1	**cup tomato purée**
1	**cup Creamed Soup Base***
½	**cup sour cream**
1	**4-ounce can diced green chilies, drained**
1	**cup shredded Monterey Jack cheese**
2	**pounds cooked shrimp**
2	**tablespoons butter**
1	**cup bread crumbs**
¾	**teaspoon chili powder**
¾	**teaspoon cumin**

*See recipe for Creamed Soup Base on page 37.

Cook rice according to directions. In large skillet, melt butter. Sauté celery and green bell pepper until soft. Add purée, soup base, sour cream, chilies and cheese. Simmer until heated. Add shrimp and rice. Transfer to a greased 9 x 13-inch baking dish. In small skillet, melt 2 tablespoons butter. Stir in bread crumbs, chili powder and cumin. Cook for 1 minute. Sprinkle mixture over casserole. Bake at 350 degrees until bubbly, about 30 minutes.

CHICKEN AND CHEESE ENCHILADA CASSEROLE

PREPARATION TIME: *2 hours*
YIELD: *12 servings*

3	**tablespoons butter**
1	**large onion, chopped**
4	**cups Creamed Soup Base***
1	**8-ounce can diced green chilies**
1	**8-ounce can salsa (or 1 cup prepared Fiesta Salsa)**
1	**4-ounce can sliced ripe olives**
½	**cup milk or chicken broth**
2	**cups sour cream**
1	**package small corn tortillas**
6	**whole chicken breasts, cooked and cut into small pieces**
1	**pound Cheddar cheese, shredded**

See recipe for Creamed Soup Base on page 37.

In large skillet, melt butter and sauté onion until soft. Add soup base, chilies, salsa, olives, milk and sour cream. Line a greased 10 x 14-inch pan with tortillas. Layer with half the soup mixture, half the chicken pieces and half the cheese. Repeat with remaining soup, chicken and cheese. Bake at 350 degrees for 30 minutes.

CARNE SECA

PREPARATION TIME: *7 hours, 30 minutes*
YIELD: *10 servings*

1	**2-pound round steak**
4	**tablespoons lard**
2	**large onions, chopped**
3	**cloves garlic, crushed**
1	**7-ounce can diced green chilies**
1	**16-ounce can chopped tomatoes**
1	**tablespoon salt**
2	**teaspoons oregano**
2	**teaspoons cumin**

Bake beef on a rimmed baking sheet at 250 degrees for about 6 hours. Turn occasionally. As juices accumulate, pour off and save. Beef must dry out slowly and completely. When beef is dried, shred in food processor or blender. Set aside. Melt lard in large skillet. Add onion and cook until soft. Add garlic and shredded meat. Stir in green chilies. Drain tomatoes, reserving liquid. Add tomatoes to skillet. Add reserved juices from beef. Season with salt, oregano and cumin. Let simmer about 30 minutes, adding the juice from the tomatoes as the liquid is absorbed.

May be served plain or as a filling for burritos or enchiladas. Use large flour or corn tortillas and 3 tablespoons Carne Seca. Roll and top with grated cheese for burritos, or top with enchilada sauce and cheese for enchiladas.

CHIMICHANGAS

PREPARATION TIME: *2 hours, 30 minutes*
YIELD: *12 servings*

4	pounds lean boneless beef (chuck or round steak)
1	onion, diced
1	clove garlic, mashed
2	tablespoons oil
1	7-ounce can green chilies
1	16-ounce can whole tomatoes
⅛	teaspoon oregano
	Salt to taste
12	medium flour tortillas
	Oil
1	head iceberg lettuce, shredded
1	cup grated cheddar cheese
1	cup sour cream
1	cup salsa

Finely dice beef. Put in cold, ungreased skillet. Cover and cook over lowest heat, undisturbed, for 2 hours, or until moisture is evaporated. Sauté onion and garlic in oil until soft. Add green chilies and cook 2-3 minutes. Drain and chop tomatoes. Reserve juice. When beef is tender and has rendered its juices, add onion mixture, oregano, salt and chopped tomatoes. Gradually add reserved tomato juice as needed during cooking. To assemble Chimichangas, place ½ cup meat mixture on a tortilla and fold envelope style. Repeat until meat mixture is used up. Preheat heavy rimmed baking sheet in 425 degree oven. Brush hot baking sheet with oil. Place Chimichangas on sheet. Brush with oil. Bake 5 minutes. Remove from oven, turn, brush with oil and return to oven. Repeat process until all sides have been cooked, about 20 minutes. Serve on a bed of shredded lettuce. Garnish with cheese, sour cream and salsa.

Meat is most flavorful if made a day ahead. Chimichangas can also be deep fried at 375 degrees until browned.

FLORES DE CARNE (STUFFED ROAST BEEF ROLLS)

PREPARATION TIME: *20 minutes*
YIELD: *4-6 servings*

1	cup peeled, chopped and cooked zucchini
1	avocado, peeled, seeded and cut into pieces
1	tablespoon minced onion
½	teaspoon chili powder
2	tablespoons oil
2	tablespoons red wine vinegar
¼	teaspoon salt
16	slices roast beef
4	large lettuce leaves

Blend zucchini and avocado until smooth. Add onion, chili powder, oil, vinegar and salt. Place a tablespoon of this mixture on each slice of roast beef. Roll up and secure with string. Line a serving dish with lettuce leaves and arrange the rolls of beef like spokes of a wheel. Remove strings before serving. Serve remaining vegetable mixture separately.

This makes an attractive platter for hors d'oeuvres or a luncheon. Garnish with radish roses and hard boiled eggs. Plain ingredients are combined to make a very interesting taste.

TOSTADA DE CARNE (MEXICAN PIZZA)

PREPARATION TIME: *45 minutes*
YIELD: *4 pizzas*

1	**pound ground beef**
½	**teaspoon salt**
1	**clove garlic, minced**
¼	**pound mushrooms, sliced**
1	**7-ounce jar green chili salsa**
4	**very large flour tortillas**
1	**tablespoon olive oil**
2	**cups chopped scallions**
2	**cups chopped green bell peppers**
1	**2-ounce can chopped black olives**
1	**pound Monterey Jack cheese, grated**
½	**cup freshly grated Parmesan cheese**
2	**medium avocados, sliced**
2	**cups sour cream**

Brown beef in skillet sprinkled with salt. Drain fat and add garlic, mushrooms and green chili salsa. Cook over high heat until liquid evaporates. Brush tortillas with oil and place on pizza pans. Spread meat sauce on tortillas. Scatter scallions, green bell peppers, olives and cheeses over top. Bake at 475 degrees until cheese melts and is bubbly, about 10 minutes. Arrange avocado slices on top. Cut into wedges and serve with sour cream.

For a complete southwestern meal, serve with Hacienda Frijoles on page 236 and Salad de Pepino Recheado on page 227.

CALABASITAS

PREPARATION TIME: *20 minutes*
YIELD: *4 servings*

½ **onion, chopped**

3 **zucchini, cut into quarters**

2 **tablespoons butter**

Salt and pepper to taste

1 **8-ounce can stewed tomatoes**

2 **cups shredded Cheddar cheese**

In large skillet, sauté onion and zucchini in butter. Season to taste. Add tomatoes. Simmer 10 minutes. Add cheese. Stir until cheese melts.

A great accompaniment to Carne Seca on page 232.

HACIENDA FRIJOLES

PREPARATION TIME: *2 hours*
YIELD: *8 servings*

1 **2-pound package pinto beans**

2 **teaspoons salt**

2 **large onions, chopped**

2 **cloves garlic, minced**

1 **16-ounce can chopped tomatoes**

1 **8-ounce can taco sauce**

1 **4-ounce can chopped green chilies, drained**

¼ **teaspoon cumin**

½ **teaspoon pepper**

Rinse beans under cold running water. Place in a large kettle and cover with cold water to 2 inches above beans. Add salt and bring to a boil. Lower heat and simmer, covered, for 1 hour. Stir in onions, garlic, tomatoes, taco sauce, green chilies, cumin and pepper until well blended. Return to a boil. Lower heat and simmer until beans are tender, about 1 hour.

VEGETABLE BURRITOS WITH AVOCADO SAUCE

PREPARATION TIME: *30 minutes*
YIELD: *16 servings*

BURRITOS
¼ **cup oil**

2 **cloves garlic, minced**

2 **medium onions, chopped**

5 **6-ounce cans sliced water chestnuts, drained**

6 **large zucchini, shredded**

1½ **pounds mushrooms, sliced**

1 **teaspoon celery salt**

4 **large tomatoes, chopped**

Salt and pepper to taste

16 **large flour tortillas**

4 **cups shredded Cheddar cheese**

AVOCADO SAUCE
2 **large avocados, peeled, pitted and chopped**

2 **cups sour cream or plain yogurt**

1 **tablespoon lemon juice**

GARNISH
16 **avocado slices**

In large skillet, heat oil over medium high heat. Add garlic and onion. Sauté until golden. Add water chestnuts and stir-fry until warm. Add zucchini and heat thoroughly. Add mushrooms and sauté briefly. Sprinkle with celery salt. Add tomatoes. Stir to heat through. DO NOT OVERCOOK - vegetables should remain firm. Remove from heat. Season to taste. Warm tortillas, one at a time, in an ungreased skillet over medium heat, turning frequently, until softened. (If tortillas are soft to begin with, this step is unnecessary.) Place 2 heaping tablespoons cheese and 2 tablespoons vegetable mixture down the center of the tortilla. Roll up and transfer to a 9 x 13-inch baking dish. Repeat with remaining tortillas. Two baking dishes will be needed. Cover dishes to prevent drying out. Bake at 350 degrees until heated through, about 15 minutes.

Mix together ingredients for Avocado Sauce. Spoon sauce down center of burritos. Place an avocado slice across the top of each burrito. Serve immediately with remaining Avocado Sauce.

Excellent buffet fare. These burritos are filling enough for a luncheon or light supper.

ENCHILADAS VERDES

PREPARATION TIME: *30 minutes*
YIELD: *6 servings*

12 small corn tortillas

Oil

3 cups green chili sauce

6 cups shredded lettuce

2 cups grated sharp Cheddar cheese

1 medium onion, chopped

2 tablespoons olive oil

2 8-ounce cans green chilies/ tomato sauce

½ teaspoon salt

Sour cream

Fry 1 tortilla in hot oil long enough to soften. Then immerse tortilla completely in green chili sauce and place flat on a small serving plate. Spread with 1 cup shredded lettuce. Sprinkle with 2-3 tablespoons cheese. Top with another tortilla which has been fried and dipped in sauce then topped with cheese. Prepare 5 more enchiladas on 5 more plates. In medium skillet sauté chopped onion in oil. Add green chili and tomato sauce and ½ teaspoon salt. Simmer 3 minutes. Pour over each enchilada. Top with a dollop of sour cream.

ARROZ MEXICANO (MEXICAN RICE)

PREPARATION TIME: *1 hour*
YIELD: *4-6 servings*

1 cup long grain rice

1 garlic clove

½ teaspoon salt

2 tablespoons oil

1 small onion, chopped

2 tomatoes, peeled and chopped

1 cup water

1 cup chicken broth

⅓ cup frozen peas, thawed

1 carrot, peeled, diced and cooked

½ teaspoon salt

Rinse rice in hot water, then cold water. Drain. Set aside. Mash garlic with salt to make a paste. Set aside. Heat oil in large, heavy saucepan. Add rice. Cook and stir over medium heat until lightly browned. Add onion and garlic paste. Cook and stir until onion is soft. Add tomatoes. Cook and stir until tomatoes are softened and blended into rice mixture. Add water. Cover and simmer until water is absorbed. Stir in broth, peas, carrot and ½ teaspoon salt. Cover and simmer until most of the liquid is absorbed, about 3-5 minutes. Reduce heat to low and steam until rice is tender, about 30-40 minutes.

JALAPEÑO CORN MUFFINS

PREPARATION TIME: *45 minutes*
YIELD: *18 muffins*

1½	**cups yellow cornmeal**
1	**tablespoon baking powder**
1	**tablespoon sugar**
1	**teaspoon salt**
1	**cup milk**
2	**eggs**
1	**8¾-ounce can creamed corn**
¼	**cup butter, melted**
1½	**cups grated Cheddar cheese**
3-4	**jalapeño peppers, finely chopped (or 1 4-ounce can chopped green chilies)**

Stir together cornmeal, baking powder, sugar and salt. Mix in milk, eggs, corn and butter. Add cheese and chilies. Stir just to combine. Heat 18 greased muffin tins at 425 degrees for 3-5 minutes. Remove from oven and fill each muffin cup ⅔ full wth muffin batter. Bake at 425 degrees for 20 minutes. Tops will be golden brown and muffins will be slightly moist inside.

SPANISH ROLLS

PREPARATION TIME: *1 hour*
YIELD: *14 rolls*

5	**eggs, hard boiled, peeled and chopped**
1	**4½-ounce can chopped ripe olives**
1	**4-ounce can diced green chilies**
1	**8-ounce can Spanish-style tomato sauce**
½	**cup oil**
8	**scallions, finely chopped**
¾	**pound Cheddar cheese, grated**
14	**hard French dinner rolls**

Combine all ingredients except rolls. Hollow out rolls. Stuff with filling. Wrap in brown paper. Bake at 300 degrees for 30-45 minutes.

PAN DULCE

PREPARATION TIME: *3 hours*
YIELD: *18 buns*

BUNS
1 package dry yeast

¾ cup warm water

3½ cups flour

¾ cup sugar

½ teaspoon salt

3 tablespoons butter, melted

2 eggs, slightly beaten

Dissolve yeast in water. Into medium bowl, sift flour with sugar and salt. Add yeast mixture, butter and eggs. Beat until smooth. Place dough in greased bowl. Cover and let rise in a warm place until doubled, about 1½ hours. Punch down, turn out onto a lightly floured surface. Knead until smooth and elastic. Pinch off pieces of dough and shape into smooth balls about 1¼ inches in diameter. Place balls on a greased baking sheet 2 inches apart. Press each ball down, flattening slightly.

TOPPING
1 cup sugar

1 cup flour

1 teaspoon cinnamon

⅛ teaspoon salt

½ cup butter, melted

1 egg, slightly beaten

Combine dry ingredients for topping. Mix butter with egg and add to dry ingredients. Gently spread 1 tablespoon topping on each bun. Let buns rise until doubled in bulk, about 30 minutes. Top buns with remaining topping. Bake at 400 degrees until lightly browned, about 10 minutes. Serve warm.

PAN PERDIDO

PREPARATION TIME: *1 hour, 30 minutes*
YIELD: *12 servings*

½ cup lard

2 pounds fresh masa

1 16-ounce carton cottage cheese

2 16-ounce cans creamed corn

2 teaspoons baking powder

1 teaspoon salt

3 cups shredded Monterey Jack cheese, divided into 1 cup portions

1 7-ounce can whole green chilies

In large bowl, beat lard until white and fluffy. Gradually beat in masa. Mix in cottage cheese, corn, baking powder and salt. Fold in 1 cup shredded cheese. Spread half the masa mixture in a greased 10 x 14-inch pan. Layer on green chilies and second cup of cheese. Spread on the remaining masa mixture and top with remaining cup of cheese. Bake at 350 degrees for 1 hour.

Serve with an egg dish for breakfast or brunch.

BUENOS DIAS BREAKFAST

PREPARATION TIME: *45 minutes*
YIELD: *12 servings*

10	**eggs**
½	**cup flour**
1	**teaspoon baking powder**
½	**teaspoon salt**
2	**cups cottage cheese**
1	**pound Monterey Jack cheese, shredded (or ½ pound Monterey Jack cheese plus ½ pound Cheddar cheese, shredded)**
½	**cup butter**
2	**4-ounce cans diced green chilies**

In large bowl, beat eggs. Add remaining ingredients. Mix well. Pour into a greased 9 x 13-inch baking dish. Bake at 350 degrees for 35 minutes.

PASTELES DE CACAO (COCOA CAKES)

PREPARATION TIME: *30 minutes*
YIELD: *16 cakes*

½	**cup butter**
1	**cup sugar**
3	**eggs**
¾	**cup cocoa**
1½	**cups flour**
3	**teaspoons baking powder**
⅛	**teaspoon salt**
⅔	**cup milk**
1	**teaspoon vanilla**

Beat butter until creamy. Gradually add sugar, beating until mixture is light and fluffy. Add eggs, one at a time, beating well. Sift together cocoa, flour, baking powder and salt. Add dry ingredients alternately with milk until thoroughly mixed. Mix in vanilla. Spoon batter into greased and floured muffin tins. Fill ⅔ full. Bake at 375 degrees until cake tester comes out clean, about 20 minutes. Do not overbake. Remove cakes from tins and cool on wire racks. Serve warm or cold.

KAHLUA ICE CREAM PIE

PREPARATION TIME: *20 minutes plus freezing time*
YIELD: *8-10 servings*

1	8½-ounce package chocolate wafers, finely crushed (about 40 wafers)
3	tablespoons sugar
5	tablespoons butter, melted
1	8-ounce package cream cheese, softened
¼	cup dark rum
1	quart coffee ice cream, softened
1	cup heavy cream
2	tablespoons sugar
1-2	tablespoons Kahlua
	Chocolate Scrolls*

In small bowl, combine chocolate crumbs, sugar and butter. Press into a 9-inch round cake pan and chill. In large bowl, beat cream cheese with rum until light and fluffy. Fold in ice cream. Pour into crust and freeze at least 4 hours. In chilled bowl, whip cream, sugar and Kahlua until stiff peaks form. Swirl onto top of pie. Garnish with Chocolate Scrolls. Freeze at least two hours. Let stand at room temperature about 5 minutes before serving.

See recipe for Chocolate Scrolls on page 204.

SOUTHWESTERN FLAN

PREPARATION TIME: *1 hour, 45 minutes*
YIELD: *8-10 servings*

8	egg yolks
2	13-ounce cans evaporated milk
6	egg whites
½	cup plus 2 tablespoons sugar
1	teaspoon vanilla
1	cup sugar

In large bowl, beat together egg yolks and milk. Put egg whites through sieve. Add egg whites, vanilla and ½ cup plus 2 tablespoons sugar to egg-milk mixture and blend well. Set aside. Pour 1 cup sugar into a bundt pan. Bake sugar at 400 degrees until caramelized and pan is coated, about 30 minutes. Pour egg-milk mixture into bundt pan and set pan in water bath. Bake at 350 degrees until flan is set, about 1 hour. Let cool and unmold. The caramel sauce will drip down around the flan.

Serve with strawberries or sliced kiwi. This flan is best prepared one day ahead and refrigerated in bundt pan.

ALMENDRADO

PREPARATION TIME: *6 hours*
YIELD: *8 servings*

1	**envelope unflavored gelatin**
¼	**cup cold water**
5	**egg whites**
¼	**teaspoon salt**
¾	**cup sugar**
1	**teaspoon almond extract**
½	**cup coarsely chopped blanched almonds**
	Green and red food coloring

CUSTARD SAUCE

5	**egg yolks**
½	**cup cold milk**
½	**cup sugar**
1	**teaspoon vanilla**
	Salt to taste
1½	**cups milk**

Soften gelatin in cold water for 5 minutes, then dissolve in top of double boiler. Chill until mixture begins to thicken. Beat egg whites until stiff. Add salt and sugar gradually, beating until mixture holds peaks. Beat in chilled gelatin, almond extract and half the almonds. Divide into 3 equal parts. Leave one part white, tint one green and the other pink. Sprinkle remaining almonds over the bottom of a wet 2-quart loaf pan. First spread green layer, then white layer and then pink layer. Chill until firm.

Beat egg yolks with ½ cup milk, sugar, vanilla and salt. Scald 1½ cups milk in top of double boiler. Gradually stir egg mixture into scalded milk and cook until mixture coats a metal spoon. Pour at once into a cold bowl. Chill until serving time. Unmold Almendrado and serve in slices with custard sauce. Garnish with extra almonds.

Almendrado is a light Mexican dessert resembling the Mexican flag.

MEXICAN WEDDING COOKIES

PREPARATION TIME: *1 hour, 30 minutes*
YIELD: *3 dozen*

1	**cup butter (not margarine)**
¾	**cup powdered sugar**
2	**cups flour**
1	**teaspoon vanilla**
1	**cup finely chopped pecans**
1½-2	**cups powdered sugar**

In large bowl, beat butter until fluffy. Add ¾ cup sugar, flour and vanilla. Mix well. Blend in pecans. Shape into 1-inch balls and place about 1 inch apart on baking sheet. Bake at 325 degrees until pale golden brown, about 25 minutes. Roll in remaining sugar, one at a time. Cool on wire racks. When cool, roll in sugar again.

ACKNOWLEDGEMENTS

Grateful acknowledgment is made to the following members whose contributions, diligence and hard work helped to make PURPLE SAGE AND OTHER PLEASURES become a reality.

Fuzzy Adelman
Claire Albanese
Meitchie Allen
Debbie Ashton
Molly Assenmacher
Angie Augur
Karlynn Baker
Eadie Fawcett
Bobbie Barg
Melea Bayne
Julie Beach
Joyce Becker
Patricia Benton
JoAnne Berglind
Faye Blake
Joyce Blee
Lynne Bogutz
Ann Boice
Patti Boitano
Betsy Bolding
Terri Bower
Anne Breen
Laury Browning
Jaime Burke
Connie Campbell
Susan Campisano
Tao Capps
Judy Carnes
Judy Caviglia
Diane Ceizyk
Chris Chapman
Mary Chapman Daley
Anne Chapman Lubliner
Robin Cherry
Ellen Colon
Perris Congdon
Tori Congdon
JoAnne Conrad
Madge Cox
Sandie Coykendall
Patti Crowley
Cathy Curry
Sandy Dauenhauer
Judy Davidson
Carol W. Davis
Harriet Davis
Laurie Decker
Donna Dempsey
CeCe Derickson
Carol Deschenes
Audry Diamontopoulos
Gilda Dick
Mary Kay Dinsmore
Nancy Dorson
Wilma Dowdall
Toby Drakulich
Janet Eddins
Pam Edgar

Bunny Edmonds
Caroline Ellermann
Kristin Federhar
Ann Fee
Ann Fister
Kay Forsythe
Cindy Fraser
Dee Anne Gibbons
Katie Gleason-Tsighis
Marnie Gooding
Julia Gordon
Mellie Graves
Sue Green
Mary Greene
Jeanne Guerrero
Ann Hadd
Judy Hammerton
Ruth Hannley
Michele Harbour
Sue Hardy
Charlotte Harris
Anne Hartnett
Ann Hastings
Jan Hastrieter
Nancy Hawke
Susan Hayes
Geneva Heller
Lynette Hendricks
Judi Herk
Ellen Hickle
Frances Hilkemeyer
Peggy Holleman
Valerie Housman
Sandal Hughes
Natalie Ireland
Linda Jackson
Marilyn Jacobs
Felice Jarrold
Debby Johnson
Ingrid Jordan
Cathy Katz
Debby Kennedy
Peg Kepner
Barbara Kittle
Paula Knauss
Barbara Kraus
Peggy Kusian
Robby Laidlaw
Cyndie Lanne
Nancy Larison
DeDe Leber
Carol Levine
Betty Lou Lindamood
Cathy Lipsman
Linda Lohse
Christy Long
Ricki Lundstrom
Nancy Lutich

Jennifer Luyties
Nancy Lynn
Lori Mackstaller
Leslie Maier
Sharon Markley
Kerry Marrs
Betsy Marshall
Jan Martin
Kathryn Martin
Debby Marvel
Karin Mather
Lynette Matteson
Paula Mazzocco
Ann McCalley
Constance McConnell
Joan McGarry
Kay McLoughlin
Bonnie Mehl
Debbie Mehl
Cathy Mendelsohn
Kim Metz
Holly Miner
Nancy Miniat
Emily Morrison
Grace Murphy
Marlene Musty
Krista Neis
Mary Ann Nichols
Geri Nielsen
Rebecca Nissen
Jody North
Betty Ochoa
Cynnie Ochoa
Tulla O'Dowd
Emily Osburn
Suzanne Ottey
Jean Owara
Mary Pace
Lyn Papanikolas
Gail Payne
Barbara Peck
Laurie Pemble
Mindy Penny
Susan Perkins
Nancy Phillips
Katharine Place
Sally Poore

Provisional Class of 1985

Nancy Quebedeaux
Suzanne Radcliffe
Cindy Ricker
Julie Rolle
Corky Ronstadt
Sandra Rothschild
Cris Russ
Sandy Sabalos
Antoinette Sanders
Karen Sanders

245

The Junior League of Tucson wishes to thank these friends who contributed so generously to this project.

Jean Schultz
Margaret Schwanke
Joy Semro
Moe Sieveke
Pamela Simoneaux
Virginia Simpson
Carole Smith
Marta Smith
Diane Somers
Jere Stephan
Virginia Stone
Kay Strickland
Jan Sturges
Lee Surwit
Susan Sutton-Robinson
Lisa Taussig
Danielle Thu
Elaine Thueson
Pam Tietig
Mary Touche
Per Touche
Joanne Tudor
Cindy Turner
Mary Jane Turner
Linda Vala
Susan Vermilyea
Carol Walsh
Diana Warren
Sally Weaver
Meredith Weedin
Mary Wiedman
Sherry Weiss
Sally Wenaas
Kathie White

Mary Wiedman
Trish Williamson
Brenda Wilson
Sandie Witthoft
Terry Woods
Becky Yeatts
Jo Ann Zirkel
Jan Bonwell
Elaine Brewster
Barbra Bruer-Allen
Laurie Buckelew
Susie Christy
Jan Cornelius
Marilyn Davison
Martha Dornette
Stuart Dornette
Sue Eck
Jeanne Fellows
Tina Garvin
Joan Gerdes
Mardi Giesler
Candy Grogin
Nancy Heldman
Magaret Hiskey
Candy Hooper
Stephanie Hoschaw
Heidi Jheeta
Lillian Jones
Kathy Kilbourne
Cyndie Kirk
Amy Kurzawski
Canilla Loehrer
Linda Longmire
Joan McGary

Cherry Moon
Claire Moore
Nancy Murietta
Mary Nichols
Susan O'Brien
Jean Odgers
Mary Ott
Cecilia Owen
Anne Parker
Lori Parker
Suzi Payton
Aileen Plumb
Michelle Peral
Debra Pesicka
Olive Schultz Price
Bertie Reddig
George Rosenberg
Michael Rexrode
Lois Ricker
Marie Rolle
Bonnie Rubin
Ella Selders
James P. Sfarnas
Mary Ann Shortman
Barbara Snapp
Tamra Stoller
Carol Swingle
Harriet Tiahnybin
Jan Tweed
Sandy Triebel
JoAnne Vondrick
Betty Weitman
Becky Wilson

INDEX

248

251